For licensing/copyright information, for additional copies
or for use in specialized settings contact:

Bernell L. King

Visions International
Post Office Box 14201
Greenville, SC 29610
Office 864.294.1974
E-Fax 512.727.9504
king@visionsmadereal.com

Contents

And there's more ●●●●●●➡

Implementing the Vision

Discovering the Vision & Developing the Character of a Visionary

The Visionary's Source Bookstore

Contact Visions International 📑

🗐 = Forms

MEET
Visions International

Bernell L. King has made it her life's pursuit to assist individuals in the full manifestation of their vision—the divine revelation of their personage, purpose and power in Christ Jesus. She embraces her client's vision as her own and offers proactive services customized to fit their needs. Ms. King draws from her experience in strategic planning, non-profit program development, business development and entrepreneurship to lead clients from discovery to implementation of their vision. A system of accountability and encouragement ensures focus, progress, and sound judgment in decision making. Clients develop their leadership qualities, set goals, and implement strategic plans to make their vision a reality in their family, career, business, ministry and life. Services are offered through seminars, workshops, conferences, print mediums and one-on-one coaching sessions.

Ms. King has been a member of Water of Life Christian Church, Greenville, SC for six years and served in leadership for five years. She obtained a Bachelor of Arts degree in Japanese and International Trade from Clemson University, Clemson, SC and has since worked in the coaching field for four years. Concurrently, she has offered professional development training to foreign executives and local business leaders in effective communication, intercultural training and leadership development.

Making Visionaries

Every great work, every great achievement, has been manifested through the steadfast holding of a vision. A vision gives one direction, insight into the future, motivation, and a reason for being.

Visions International equips individuals to be visionaries by helping them discover and develop their *Vision—the divine revelation of their personage, purpose, and power in Christ Jesus.*

The Mission

Our mission is to partner with individuals and aid in the full manifestation of their vision by encouraging the use of biblical principals in their day-to-day life, business operations, and relationships.

The Services

Our services entail helping clients with visioning or making their life goals a reality. Through *The Visioning Process*^{SM} clients develop a personal and business strategic plan that focuses on four core areas of vision:

- The Visionary (Personal, Professional and Leadership Development)
- The Vision (Purpose, Defining and Focusing)
- The Written Vision (Goals, Plans and Marketing the Vision)
- Implementation of the Vision (Organizational Structure, Financial Planning, Strategic Actions and Growth)

Allow us the opportunity to partner with you and see your
Vision Made Real^{SM}.

Contact us today!
Fill out the form on the final page and return it to us or write, call or email us at:

Bernell L. King
Business Coach
Post Office Box 14201
Greenville, SC 29610
Office 864.294.1974
E-Fax 512.727.9504
king@visionsmadereal.com

"I have worked in many facets of retail and have held numerous leadership roles. I have the necessary expertise to successfully operate my own business. The class permitted me to gain expert knowledge into the

Knowledgeable

process of becoming a business owner. Thank you!"

Motivating

". . . After completing the workshop I became so pumped up to pursue my vision. I couldn't stopped telling people about you and . . . the encouragement you showered on us through out the classes. [Two years later] I keep asking myself over and over why I feel so unfulfilled and . . . the answer keeps on popping in my head that I need the right guidance. I'm always skeptical to just go out there and seek the help I need so I just do my work which speaks for itself, hence bringing in more work. I am at a point now that I know my full vision is not in use and that's where you come in . . ."

Encouraging

"This class was very motivational to me. To help me begin to write the vision; present it first to God for wisdom and knowledge of how to pursue this vision, then to present it to the bank. Also, this class helped me to start encouraging myself by networking with the other lady entrepreneurs."

Informative

"The workshop was very informative and extremely helpful. I have not yet decided which business I will pursue but whatever road I choose, I have the very necessary tools to travel with."

Enjoyable

"I thoroughly enjoyed the class. Bernell is very well versed, interesting and knowledgeable. I'm excited this program is available. Thank you."

I Believe

"Thanks for a great seminar about business. I'm wiser about many things in business because of you. Your encouragement helped me to believe that I can run a small business."

DEFINING THE VISION

"Not that I have already attained, or am already perfected; but I press on, that I may lay hold of that for which Christ Jesus has also laid hold of me."
Philippians 3:12

DEFINING YOUR MISSION AND VISION STATEMENT

Every organization, whether for profit or non-profit, big or small needs a mission statement as a source of direction. A mission statement is the compass that lets leaders, employees, customers, stakeholders and stockholders know your company's position and where it's headed. Your mission statement provides the focus on one vision for the entire organization and everyone involved.

Companies and people share certain characteristics. Over time, both develop personalities that motivate their actions and shape their way of life, values, and beliefs. Without a purpose or a mission both a person and a company are subject to falter.

The mission . . .

- Shapes the identity of your company, its purpose, its focus, and its ultimate goal.
- Communicates the kind of company you are.
- Gives your company a sense of purposefulness and provides a reason for working other than compensation.
- Unifies the people in your company by providing a common focus and common goal especially if the people have diverse backgrounds and your company is international in scope.
- Guides your decision-making, actions, and words.
- Provides a foundation upon which your company can build its future.
- Endures and becomes a natural part of your work.

How does a mission statement vary from all this other stuff I've heard of?

A Vision Statement, Business Philosophy, Objectives, Values, Strategies, Pledge, Tactics, Purpose, Promise, Beliefs, Standards, Code of Ethics, Idea, Call to Action, Guidelines, Direction, Focus, Commitment, Policy, Discipline, Covenant, Standards of Performance, or Credo?

These various statements are not synonymous. They vary individually in premise and tone. I personally feel that no two should replace the vision and the mission. Without a vision, the people perish. The vision is the company's pursuit, while the mission is how the company will accomplish it. Depending on your company and what you would like to communicate to your audience, you may choose to compliment your vision and mission with other statements.

The Vision

Every great work, every great achievement, has been manifested through the steadfast holding of a vision. A vision gives one direction, insight into the future, motivation, and a reason for being. The vision of a company is the description of a picture of the organization at some time in the future. The vision sets the overall direction of your company. It's what your company strives to be. The vision is written in future-oriented terms that describe the nature and persona of your company.

The Values

Values are the collective principles and ideals that guide the thoughts, actions, and motives of an individual or group of individuals. Values define the character and standards of your company.

DEFINING YOUR MISSION AND VISION STATEMENT

The Mission

The mission statement specifies a company's purpose and "reason for being". It is the primary objective by which all plans and programs are fashioned; therefore, it should reflect stakeholders' needs and shared values. The mission is to be accomplished while the vision is to be pursued. The mission is written in action-oriented terms that communicate how and what you will do to become the company stated in your vision statement. The mission could include stated boundaries of your core services, target groups, and target geographical regions.

The Business Philosophy

The business philosophy sets the "rule of conduct" for operating the organization. It uses concrete descriptions of how the values of the organization will be applied to operate the business.

Technical Writing

The uniqueness of a company should be portrayed in its mission statement. There are many ways to compose, present, and distribute a mission statement and each company's methods will be different. The differences stem from the four basic elements of a mission statement: target audience, length, tone, and format.

- *Target Audience*
  Who is the mission statement intended for? The general public? Employees? Stockholders? Investors? All audiences? When writing, you can address each audience separately (To Our Customers, To Our Employees). The target audience can also be specifically mentioned in the statement. For example, "we are the store for middle-income women with children." The target audience will determine the length, tone and visibility of your mission statement.

- *Length*
  There are no set rules for length. For some companies, one line is sufficient but others may have an extensive document with a mission, vision, values, etc. Some are longer than one line but within a page. The bottom line is that the mission should be long enough to reach the target audience but be sure your audience can identify and understand your purpose.

- *Tone*
  Tone is the crucial element that should be strategically designed to resonate with your audience. Decide whether your statement should be conversational, formal, or written by the president. Remember, to take into consideration your company and your target audience. The language you employ should also be carefully considered because you do not want to create a statement that inadequately represents your company and its purpose. For example, the use of haughty language may cause your statement not to be taken seriously.

Title, key words and phrases greatly influence the tone. Instead of the headline "Mission Statement", companies have added their own character with titles such as "Our Way to Excellence", "Strategic Vision", and "This We Believe". Here is an abbreviated list of common key words and phrases.

Accomplished	Direct	Initiative	Productivity
Asset	Employee	Leader	Reliable
Change	Empower	Long-term	Return on equity
Commitment	Enthusiasm	Mutual	Risk
Conscience	Fun	Passion	Security
Dedication	Growth	Performance	Tomorrow
Dignity	Harmony	Principles	Value

For more ideas and insight on composing vision and mission statements, view actual statements from other companies and organizations.

Sample Mission and Vision Statements

- **Visions International, Greenville, SC:** "The mission of Visions International is to partner with individuals and aid in the full manifestation of their vision by encouraging the use of biblical principals in their day-to-day life, business operations and relationships.
- **Water of Life Christian Church, Greenville, SC:** "The mission of Water of Life Christian Church is to preach the good news of Jesus Christ, minister reconciliation, make disciples, and prepare them for kingdom purpose."
- **Whitney Museum:** "To preserve collect, and exhibit 20th century American Art"
- **In Touch Magazine, Atlanta, GA:** "To inspire, encourage, educate, and change lives by communicating God's Truth, and to connect people to God's work through In Touch Ministries.
- **SHARE, Upstate, SC:** "Our mission is to help low-income individuals, families, and neighborhoods become self-sufficient. We serve families whose annual incomes are at or below poverty level as defined by federal guidelines. Services are provided based on need and our ability to help without regard to race, color, creed, or gender. Overall, about half of our clients are white, half non-white, two-thirds female, and one-third male. The primary catalyst mission of SHARE is to make the entire community more responsive to the needs and aspirations of the poor by mobilizing all available resources toward the goal of human advancement, of assisting low-income citizens break the cycle of poverty and become self-sufficient.
- **Franklin Covey:** "The mission of Franklin Covey is to help you ignite the power of your people to achieve breakthrough results."
- **Academy for Coach Training (ACT): Vision** – "We are compassionate champions of the human spirit and visionary catalysts for personal and organizational transformation". **Mission** – "We deliver innovative, unparalleled coach training, products, and services, empowering a thriving community of successful coaches, clients, and associates."

See other company and organization websites or documents for sample statements or refer to the cited source below.

Source: "The Mission Statement Book: 301 Corporate Mission Statements" by Jeffrey Abrahams

The Benefits of Setting Goals

Goal setting is a powerful procedure that gives you long-term vision and short-term motivation. At its simplest level the process of setting goals and targets allows you to plan where you want to go in life. If you know where you want to go, you know what you have to concentrate on and improve.

When you set clearly defined, written goals, you can measure and take pride in the achievement of those goals. You can:

- ✓ Achieve more
- ✓ Improve performance
- ✓ Increase your motivation to achieve
- ✓ Eliminate attitudes that hinder your progress
- ✓ Improve your self-confidence
- ✓ Increase your pride and satisfaction in your achievements

Research has shown that people who set and achieve their goals:

- ✓ Suffer less from stress and anxiety
- ✓ Concentrate better
- ✓ Show more self-confidence
- ✓ Perform better
- ✓ Are happier and more satisfied

The process of achieving goals and seeing their achievement gives you the confidence and self-belief that you are capable of achieving higher and more difficult goals.

Provided you have the self-discipline to carry it through, goal setting can be easy. The following section on goal setting will give you effective guidelines to help you to use this technique effectively.

Your Action List

1. Envision the largest vision you can.
2. Write down specifics of that vision.
3. Establish a specific date to achieve your goals.
4. Establish specific milestones to the goal.
5. Get started, even if it is unclear and the end looks impossible.
6. Constantly ask yourself, "Is what I am doing right now the best I can be doing to reach my goals?"
7. Concentrate on doing what gets you closer to those goals. Ask yourself, "Is what I'm doing right now a step towards the accomplishment of my goals?"
8. Avoid naysayers, time wasters, and irrelevant activity.
9. Be on the lookout for, and be prepared to seize any opportunities that arise.

Thinking A Goal Through

When you are thinking about how to achieve your goals, ask the following questions to help you focus on the sub-goals or steps that lead to the achievement of the main goal.

- ✓ What skills do I need to achieve this?
- ✓ What information and knowledge do I need?
- ✓ What help, assistance, or collaboration is necessary?
- ✓ What resources do I need?
- ✓ What can block progress?
- ✓ Am I making any assumptions?
- ✓ Is there a better way of doing things?

Think about how your life is going right now – at home, at work, at school, or with friends. Ask yourself the following questions:

1. How do I feel about my life – am I happy? Sad? Confused?
2. If I had to describe my life to someone in just one sentence, what would I say?
3. Is there a part of my life that I'd like to be different? How do I propose I change it?
4. What can I do to make this happen?
5. Now, pretend it's one year later. What am I doing now? What's different in my life?
6. How did I get there?
7. Now, pretend it's three years later. What am I doing?
8. Am I in school? What am I studying?
9. What changes have occurred in my life during these last 3 years?
10. How do I feel right now?

Decide what will help you get to where your imagination just took you, set your goals, and make it happen!

Source: Unknown

Area of Life (circle one) *Self, Family, Spiritual, Emotional, Career, Business, Ministry, Health, Financial*		
Today's Date	**Priority** **A B C**	**Goal:**
Benefits/Rewards		
Possible Obstacles		
Time Frame		

Step	Objective To Do	Completion Date
1		
2		
3		
4		
5		

Evaluate Progress:

BUSINESS START-UP CHECKLIST ● ● ● ● ● ●

Writing the Vision

☐ Vision Statement _____

☐ Mission Statement _____

☐ Personal Strategic Vision Plan _____

☐ Get a Mentor/Hire a Coach _____

☐ Business Plan _____

    The Company Summary _____

    The Marketing Summary _____

    The Financial Management Summary _____

    The Management Summary _____

    The Executive Summary _____

    Supporting Documents (If applicable) _____

      Tax Returns of principals for the last 3 years _____

      Personal Financial Statement _____

      Franchised Business - Copy of franchise contract and all supporting
        documents provided by the franchisor _____

      Copy of proposed lease or purchase agreement for building space _____

      Copy of resumes or curriculum vitae of all principals _____

      Copies of letters of intent from suppliers _____

☐ Prepare a Training Manual for Employees _____

☐ Business Strategic Vision Plan _____

Implementing the Vision

Start-up

☐ Check with the Secretary of State to see if your business name is available _____

☐ Register Business Name (Clerk of Court) _____

☐ Business License (City Hall of all municipalities where business is conducted) _____

☐ Federal Tax ID (Form SS4) _____

☐ Retail License _____

☐ Wholesale License _____

☐ South Carolina Tax Commission _____

☐ Employer Withholding Number (if you have employees) _____

☐ Insurance (liability, casualty, worker's compensation, etc.) _____

☐ Other Required Licensing or Registration (OSHA, professional, etc.) _____

☐ Legal Form of Business (consult an attorney or accountant if necessary
   and file proper documentation with Secretary of State) _____

☐ Zoning Approval _____

☐ Real Estate transactions may require special consideration, get legal advice _____

☐ Occupancy Permits _____

☐ Register Trademarks and/or Service Marks (Secretary of State) _____

☐ Obtain a Copyright or Patent Registration if applicable (US Department
   of Commerce and Copyright Office of the Library of Congress) _____

☐ Obtain a Bar Code or Universal Product Code (UPC) _____

BUSINESS START-UP CHECKLIST ●●●●●●

To Accomplish   *Date Accomplished*

Financing the Vision
Finances

- [ ] Personal Credit - obtain all three credit reports before approaching a bank _____
- [ ] Accountant - get advise on bookkeeping system _____
- [ ] Bookkeeping System _____
- [ ] Business Budget _____
- [ ] Business Bank Account _____
- [ ] Compensation and wages for owners, personnel, and contractors _____
- [ ] Develop a competitive rate structure for products/services _____
- [ ] Develop a billing system _____
- [ ] Receipt Book to document sales and provide to customers _____
- [ ] Keep track of all receipts of all tax deductible expenses and mileage _____
      with explanations of expenses (consult an accountant)
- [ ] Credit card merchants (if you will accept credit cards consult your bank's _____
      Merchant Bankcard Services, retail banker)

Communicating the Vision
Marketing and Advertising

- [ ] Develop a consistent image _____
   - Logo _____
   - Color Scheme _____
   - Fonts _____
- [ ] Motto or Tag Line (i.e. "we do chicken right") _____
- [ ] Business Cards _____
- [ ] Flyers, Brochure, Postcards* _____
- [ ] Local phonebook listing, newspaper ad, radio, TV* _____

Affiliations - Personal and Professional

- [ ] Networking - network casually and formally by participating _____
      in local business networking clubs and events
- [ ] Join local and national associations in your field _____
- [ ] Consider membership with the local Chamber of Commerce _____
- [ ] Keep an updated copy of your resume or cirriculum vitae _____

*These types of advertising are not for every business. Be sure to explore other forms of advertising specific to your target market that will give you the greatest return on your marketing investment.

BUSINESS START-UP CHECKLIST ●●●●●●

To Accomplish   *Date Accomplished*

Writing the Vision

- [ ] Vision Statement   _____
- [ ] Mission Statement   _____
- [ ] Personal Strategic Vision Plan   _____
- [ ] Get a Mentor/Hire a Coach   _____
- [ ] Business Plan   _____
  The Company Summary   _____
  The Marketing Summary   _____
  The Financial Management Summary   _____
  The Management Summary   _____
  The Executive Summary   _____
  Supporting Documents (If applicable)   _____
    Tax Returns of principals for the last 3 years   _____
    Personal Financial Statement   _____
    Franchised Business - Copy of franchise contract and all supporting   _____
       documents provided by the franchisor
    Copy of proposed lease or purchase agreement for building space   _____
    Copy of resumes or curriculum vitae of all principals   _____
    Copies of letters of intent from suppliers   _____
- [ ] Prepare a Training Manual for Employees   _____
- [ ] Business Strategic Vision Plan   _____

Implementing the Vision

Start-up

- [ ] Check with the Secretary of State to see if your business name is available   _____
- [ ] Register Business Name (Clerk of Court)   _____
- [ ] Business License (City Hall of all municipalities where business is conducted)   _____
- [ ] Federal Tax ID (Form SS4)   _____
- [ ] Retail License   _____
- [ ] Wholesale License   _____
- [ ] South Carolina Tax Commission   _____
- [ ] Employer Withholding Number (if you have employees)   _____
- [ ] Insurance (liability, casualty, worker's compensation, etc.)   _____
- [ ] Other Required Licensing or Registration (OSHA, professional, etc.)   _____
- [ ] Legal Form of Business (consult an attorney or accountant if necessary   _____
      and file proper documentation with Secretary of State)
- [ ] Zoning Approval   _____
- [ ] Real Estate transactions may require special consideration, get legal advice   _____
- [ ] Occupancy Permits   _____
- [ ] Register Trademarks and/or Service Marks (Secretary of State)   _____
- [ ] Obtain a Copyright or Patent Registration if applicable (US Department   _____
      of Commerce and Copyright Office of the Library of Congress)
- [ ] Obtain a Bar Code or Universal Product Code (UPC)   _____

BUSINESS START-UP CHECKLIST ●●●●●●

Financing the Vision
Finances

- ☐ Personal Credit - obtain all three credit reports before approaching a bank
- ☐ Accountant - get advise on bookkeeping system
- ☐ Bookkeeping System
- ☐ Business Budget
- ☐ Business Bank Account
- ☐ Compensation and wages for owners, personnel, and contractors
- ☐ Develop a competitive rate structure for products/services
- ☐ Develop a billing system
- ☐ Receipt Book to document sales and provide to customers
- ☐ Keep track of all receipts of all tax deductible expenses and mileage with explanations of expenses (consult an accountant)
- ☐ Credit card merchants (if you will accept credit cards consult your bank's Merchant Bankcard Services, retail banker)

Communicating the Vision
Marketing and Advertising

- ☐ Develop a consistent image
    - Logo
    - Color Scheme
    - Fonts
- ☐ Motto or Tag Line (i.e. "we do chicken right")
- ☐ Business Cards
- ☐ Flyers, Brochure, Postcards*
- ☐ Local phonebook listing, newspaper ad, radio, TV*

Affiliations - Personal and Professional

- ☐ Networking - network casually and formally by participating in local business networking clubs and events
- ☐ Join local and national associations in your field
- ☐ Consider membership with the local Chamber of Commerce
- ☐ Keep an updated copy of your resume or cirriculum vitae

*These types of advertising are not for every business. Be sure to explore other forms of advertising specific to your target market that will give you the greatest return on your marketing investment.

LEGAL FORMS OF BUSINESS ●●●●●●●

When organizing a new business, one of the most important decisions will be choosing the structure of the business. Factors influencing your decision include:

Legal restrictions	Capital needs
Liabilities assumed	Number of employees
Type of business operation	Tax advantages or disadvantages
Earnings distribution	Length of business operation

The advantages and disadvantages of a sole proprietorship, partnerships and corporations are listed below. Following these explanations, you will find a chart that gives a quick look at each form of ownership.

Sole Proprietorship

This is the easiest and least costly way of starting a business. Opening the door for business can form a sole proprietorship. There are likely to be fees to obtain business name registration, a fictitious name certificate and other necessary licenses. Attorney's fees for starting the business will be less than the other business forms because less preparation of documents is required. The owner has absolute authority over all business decisions; therefore, the owner is personally responsible for the results of all decisions and debt incurred by the business.

Partnership

There are several types of partnerships of which the two most common types being the *General* and *Limited Partnerships*. A partnership can be formed simply by an oral agreement between two or more persons but a written, legal partnership agreement is highly recommended and can be drawn up by an attorney. Legal fees for drawing up a partnership agreement are higher than those for a sole proprietorship, but may be lower than incorporating. A partnership agreement could be helpful in assigning responsibilities, establishing protocol for major decision making and solving any disputes. However, partners are responsible for the other partner's business actions, as well as their own.

A Partnership Agreement should include the following:

- ✓ Type of business
- ✓ Amount of equity invested by each partner
- ✓ Division of profit or loss
- ✓ Partners' compensation
- ✓ Distribution of assets on dissolution
- ✓ Duration of partnership
- ✓ Provisions for changes or dissolving the partnership
- ✓ Dispute settlement clause restrictions of authority and expenditures
- ✓ Settlement in case of death or incapacitation

General Partnership

Under a general partnership, each partner is liable for all debts of the business and all profits are taxed as income to the partners based on their percentage of ownership. A general partnership, like a sole proprietorship, registers a business name with the Clerk of Court in the county/city in which the business is located.

LEGAL FORMS OF BUSINESS

Limited Partnership

A Limited Partnership is also established by an agreement between two or more individuals. The difference is there are two types of partners, a *general partner* and a *limited partner*. The general partner has greater control in some aspects of the partnership; only a general partner can decide to dissolve the partnership. General partners have no limitations on the dividends they can receive from profit but consequently incur unlimited liability. Limited partners can only receive a share of profits based on the prorated amount on their investment and their liability, with the exception of those participating in management, is proportional to their investment.

Corporation

A business may incorporate without an attorney, but legal advice is highly recommended. The corporate structure is usually the most complex and most costly to organize. The following characteristics distinguish a corporation from other forms of business:

- ✓ *Capital.* Capital can be raised through the sale of stock.
- ✓ *Decision Makers.* Corporations are comprised of three groups of people: shareholders, directors, and officers.
- ✓ *Ownership.* A corporation can be owned by non-US residents, business entities or individuals, except corporations with Subchapter "S" status.
- ✓ *Stock.* Control depends on stock ownership. Persons with the largest stock ownership, not the total number of shareholders, control the corporation. With control of stock shares or 51 percent of stock, a person or group is able to make policy decisions.
- ✓ *Decision-making.* Control is exercised through regular board of directors' meetings and annual stockholders' meetings. Legally, records must be kept to document decisions made by the board of directors. Small, closely held corporations can operate more informally, but record keeping cannot be eliminated.
- ✓ *Liability.* Officers of a corporation can be liable to stockholders for improper actions. Although a corporation has the advantage of limited liability it is not total protection from lawsuits. Liability is generally limited to stock ownership, except where fraud is involved.
- ✓ *Separate Legal Entity.* The corporation can own assets, borrow money and perform business functions without the direct involvement of the owner(s) of the corporation.
- ✓ *Life of the Corporation.* A corporation can endure after the death of an owner or when a partner leaves.
- ✓ *Double Taxation.* Corporations are subject to "double taxation" because corporate earnings are taxed and stockholder dividends are taxed. An alternate avenue to double taxation is a Subchapter S Corporation.

General Corporation (C Corporation)

This is the most common business structure and is most appropriate for companies planning to have more than 30 stockholders or large public stock offerings. General Corporations may choose to elect Subchapter S status.

LEGAL FORMS OF BUSINESS

Close Corporation (Statutory Close Corporation)

This option is well suited for the individual starting a company alone or with a small group of people. Stockholders are limited to a maximum of 30 people but one person can hold all the stock. Some advantages are reduced paperwork and requirements that are burdensome for smaller businesses. Establishment as a Closed Corporation alleviates bylaws, a board of directors, and annual shareholders meetings, but a shareholder management agreement and other operational agreements are required. Not all states recognize a Close Corporation so in this case, Subchapter S status is an option.

Subchapter "S" Corporation

An Internal Revenue Code permits a corporation to avoid "double taxation" by allowing the owners to report income or losses as thought they were "partners". Therefore, profits and losses are taxed at the individual rate instead of the corporate rate and reported on the owners' personal returns. Before qualifying for S Corporation status, a General or Close Corporation must be formed first and all shareholders must be citizens or permanent residents of the United States. See IRS publication 589.

Non-profit Corporation/Non-Stock

For individuals or groups seeking "non-profit", tax exempt status.

Professional Corporation (PC)

This entity is reserved for businesses that require professional licensure, such as doctors, dentist, attorneys, engineers, and architects. Most states require proof of professional license, a statement of purpose and additional fees beyond a General Corporation. PCs generally take longer to form.

Limited Liability Company (LLC) and Limited Liability Partnership (LLP)

An LLC is a hybrid between a corporation and a partnership while still maintaining status as a legal entity distinct from its owners. As a separate legal entity, it can acquire assets, incur liabilities, and conduct business. It provides limited liability for the owners. The LLC owners risk only their investment and personal assets are not at risk. Like a S Corporation, an LLC's profits and losses are reflected on the owner's personal income tax returns. One thing that distinguishes a LLC from a corporation is that an LLC does not issue stock, they are owned by *membership interest* meaning there are "Members", not partners and stockholders. LLCs are also not required to hold annual meetings.

The LLP is similar to the LLC except that it is aimed at professional organizations.

Determining the Initial Directors (Corporation), Members or Managers (LLC)

In most states, only one director is required for a corporation. For LLCs, two managers or members may be required.

LEGAL FORMS OF BUSINESS ●●●●●●

Incorporating in Other States

If you plan to do business outside of your home state, you can elect to form a corporation in a different state for the purpose of reduced fees, paperwork, restrictions, or taxes. If you are not planning to do business in other states, it is best to form the corporation in your home state. For more information regarding these options, consult your attorney.

Registered Agent

Most states require corporations and Limited Liability Companies (LLCs) to maintain a designated person or entity (a resident of the state of corporation) to be responsible for receiving vital legal and tax documents on behalf of the corporation. This agent has to be officially registered with the state.

Source: The Corporation Company- www.incorporate.com, Small Business Administration – "Small Business Resource Guide 2001".

LEGAL FORMS OF BUSINESS AT A GLANCE

Type of Entity	Main Advantages	Main Drawbacks
Sole Proprietorship	Easiest and least expensive to create and operate Owner reports profit or loss on his or her personal tax return	Owner personally liable for business debts
General Partnership	Simple and less expensive to create and operate than a corporation Owners (partners) report their share of profit or loss on their personal tax returns	Owners (partners) personally liable for business debts
Limited Partnership	Limited partners have limited personal liability for business debts as long as they don't participate in management General partners can raise cash without involving outside investors in management of business	General partners are personally liable for business debts More expensive to create than general partnership
General Corporation (C Corporation)	Owners have limited personal liability for business debts Fringe benefits can be deducted as a business expense Owners can split corporate profit among owners and corporation, paying lower overall tax rate	More expensive to create than partnership or sole proprietorship Owners must meet legal requirements for stock registration and paperwork Separate taxable entity
Subchapter Corporation (S Corporation)	Owners have limited personal liability for business debts Owners report their share of corporate profit or loss on their personal tax returns. Owners can use corporate loss to offset income from other sources Avoid "double taxation" with a simpler tax structure that passes income through to owner	More expensive to create than partnership or sole proprietorship Owners must meet legal requirements for registration and paperwork Income must be allocated to owners according to their ownership interests Fringe benefits limited for owners who own more than 2% of shares
Limited Liability Partnership	Owners have no personal liability for malpractice of other owners	More expensive to create than partnership or sole proprietorship Owners must meet legal requirements for registration
Non-profit Corporation	Corporation doesn't pay income taxes; contributions to charitable corporation are tax-deductible Fringe benefits can be deducted as a business expense	Full tax advantages are available only to groups organized for charitable, scientific, educational, literary or religious purposes Property transferred to corporation stays there; if corporation ends, property must go to another nonprofit
Limited Liability Company (LLC)	Owners have limited personal liability for business debts even if they participate in management. Protection of personal assets Profit and loss can be allocated differently than ownership interests Can choose between being taxed as a partnership or corporation	More expensive to create than partnership or sole proprietorship State laws for creating LLCs may not reflect latest federal tax changes

WRITING THE VISION

Take a Sigh of Relief
Writing a business plan is by no means painless, but it's only as complicated as you make it. Unlike grant applications, business plans have liberties and no set format. However, there are unalterable components, such as the financial statements, the market analysis, and the executive summary. Your plan does not have to be a thesis or complex business executive document but it should have a professional appearance with supported reasoning. It should clearly and concisely inform your reader about you, your business and its profit-making potential. There is no need to show how much you know or use lofty language. Don't include topics just because they are in the business plan outline; they may not apply to your business. *Your plan should be targeted, relevant and realistic.*

Why do I need a business plan?
Typically, investors (banks or private investors) will review the *Executive Summary* and the financial statements at most. But the remainder of the plan is just as important because it is how you were able to devise such conclusions about your business' profitability. It is also there for further information and explanation if the reader should need it.

The business plan is not solely to procure funds but to guide you in planning the launch, operation, and growth of your company. This is another reason why a thorough and useful plan is necessary.

Be encouraged! Everybody knows it's just a plan but make it a good one! Here are some tips on writing a successful business plan.

The Greatest Tip!

▪ **YOUR WORDS NEED TO TURN IN TO MONEY!**

The Rest of the Tips (Important, nonetheless)

▪ **Money is not given away based on need.** Everyone seeking for funds will have a need. The key is providing an unequivocal business plan of your product and/or service and how you plan to make a return on investment. Not to mention the experience and expertise to back it up.

▪ **Avoid jargon.** The reader may not be familiar with the language in your field so you want your plan to be clear, easily understood, and reader-friendly. Accepted acronyms or terminology in your field may not be known to the reader; therefore you will want to avoid having them search to find meanings. Even worse, if you haven't told them the meaning the first time you used it.

▪ **Be positive.** Don't say "we feel" or "we hope." Say "we know," or "our experience has shown." Use "can" and "will" over "may" and "might."

▪ **Be brief.** Follow the instructions (specific loan programs) and don't be wordy. Make clear, concise, and targeted points. A business plan can be as many pages as you need to prove the profitability and viability of your business idea but don't get carried away.

▪ **Use simple formatting.** For example, 10 or 12 point font, standard fonts, line spacing. Bold type is easier to read than all capital letters, underlining, or italics. Bolding is also used to create emphasis. Therefore, excessive bolding loses its meaning and fatigues the reader. You may use graphs, charts, color, etc. but be sure to maintain a proper balance between text and graphics.

TIPS ON BUSINESS PLAN WRITING ⬤⬤⬤⬤⬤⬤

- **Use appendices and attachments for necessary and relevant documents.** Possible attachments may be financial statements, tax documents, supplier and lease agreements, and resumes.

- **Avoid over qualifiers.** For example, very unique and very excellent.

- **Avoid needless qualifiers.** For example, many, partially, really, rather, seldom, sometimes, somewhat, and very.

- **Use simple language and simple sentence construction.**

- **Use action words instead of forms of the verbs "to be" and "to have."**

- **Personalize your plan by using active voice instead of passive voice.** For example, "It was decided . . ." or "Plans were drawn up . . ." Instead, "We decided . . ." or "We drew up plans . . ." Passive voice makes the plan less interesting and dull.

- **Proofread.** Have someone proofread and edit for spelling, syntax, and grammar. Spell check on your computer doesn't catch all mistakes.

- **Avoid making unsupported assumptions or statements** (*This is a Big One!*). Reread carefully and remove them or support them with accredited sources, statistics, and/or references.

- **Be compelling, but don't overestimate your case.**

- **Be realistic in presenting your business.** Do not overstate your need, the projected outcomes, or basic facts about your business or industry. It is dangerous to promise more than you can deliver.

- **Keep it simple.** Eliminate wordiness. Edit your text for any unnecessary words, ideas, or information.

- **Avoid cute titles or clever acronyms.** They don't win any points. They waste your time creating them and run the risk of irritating the reader.

- **Information too generic or too broad will not help.** National figures, trends, or generalizations may not support your target market. The reader needs to know about the people you are trying to reach and your location.

- **Avoid overstatement or emotional appeals.**

- **Avoid circular reasoning.** "The problem is we have no computers. Buying computers will solve this problem."

- **What you want to achieve is:**

  1. a demonstration that you have a thorough understanding of your product and/or service, the problem you plan to solve, and your market.

  2. a demonstration that your service and financial goals are realistic, measurable and attainable.

  3. a demonstration that your idea is viable and will generate the growth needed to sustain.

  4. a demonstration that you have the people and experience to make it happen.

  5. a demonstration that it is the same problem the investor seeks to address (applicable for targeted funding opportunities).

TIPS ON BUSINESS PLAN WRITING ●●●●●●

- **Goals**

    1. Goals are broad statements of overall purposes. It points to the direction you are headed.

    2. Most plans are based on one, two or three goals. Over three goals and the plan begins to appear less focused.

    3. Goals represent an ideal or hoped for state. As such, they are not generally attainable over the short term. Probably not in the time frame of your plan.

- **Objectives**

    1. Objectives are the actions taken to attain the goals. Each goal should have one or more objectives which, when accomplished, will collectively achieve your goal.

    2. Objectives are specific, achievable, measurable statements about what is going to be accomplished within a certain amount of time.

- **Narrative**

    1. The blueprint for how and when things are to be accomplished.

    2. The action plan for your objectives and rationale for the selection of your approach.

    3. Your objectives should be the foundation and guide for presenting your plan. There should be methods and strategies described for meeting each objective.

    4. Methods should appear doable; otherwise you lose creditability.

    5. The roles of the owners and other key decision makers should be explained along with some statements of their creditability. Resumes may also be included in the appendix.

    6. A timeline may be helpful in planning task completion or phases of the business.

- **Budget**

    1. Your budget describes required resources for operation of the business. Every expense should be necessary for operation. Include a brief narrative on how much money you are requesting and the main resources it will be used for (i.e. salaries and equipment).

    2. If a form is provided, use the form.

    3. Get help form your accountant or the Small Business Development Center (SBDC).

- **Executive Summary**

    Your executive summary should effectively summarize and highlight key information about your business. This is your moment to convince the investor so choose your words wisely because you only have one and a half pages at the most. Be sure to include:

    1. a statement about your company (mission, goals, business ownership and legal structure).

    2. what your product/service is, the problem it will solve and how much money it will make.

    3. the advantage you and your business have over your competitors.

    4. a brief statement about you and your partner's skills and experience.

    5. how much you need and a brief explanation of what you plan to use it for.

Adapted from "Tips for Writing Successful Grants" Compiled by Leon F. Temples

THE BUSINESS PLAN – THE BOTTOM LINE ●●●●●●

This is a simplified business plan outline which highlights the key components of all business plans in simplified terms. If you choose to start with this outline, thoroughly address these questions and you will have a business plan to guide you in the implementation and growth of your business vision.

1. Describe the business that you would like to start. Your mission statement. [Use photos from magazines]

WHAT?

2. What is your primary occupation? That is, what kind of work do you usually do? For example, clerical, computer programming, construction, etc. [Include a resume]

3. Describe any prior training or experience in the type of business that you are considering. [include certificates and diplomas]

WHERE?

4. Where will you operate your business?

FOR WHO?

5. Who do you expect to be the consumer/users of your product or service?

HOW?

6. How will you attract those customers or clients? [Include sample ads, flyers, brochures]

WHEN?

7. In order to break even, in addition to the personal income mentioned above, your business will have to generate revenue to cover business expenses and to pay taxes. How many months do you think will be needed before your business is able to earn enough revenue to cover all personal, business and tax expenses?

HOW MUCH?

8. Where do you expect to get the money to cover your personal and business expenses prior to your business generating adequate revenue – (i.e. savings, bank loan, second mortgage or home equity loan, friends/relatives, credit cards, local/regional funds, other)? Please specify. What is the price of your product/service? Four main elements that determine pricing: (1) material and supplies, (2) labor and operating expenses, (3) planned profit and (4) competition.

9. If you expect a bank loan, what personal assets do you have that could serve as collateral for such a loan (i.e. house, car, stocks, bonds, personal property, inventory list(s))?

WITH WHOM?

10. How many employees, other than yourself, will you have initially? Eventually? [Include job descriptions]

BUSINESS PLAN OUTLINE ●●●●●●

1.0 Executive Summary

The executive summary should not exceed two typewritten pages. The executive summary should encapsulate your entire plan with emphasis on major highlights to peak your reader's attention and draw $$$. Therefore, it is best to write it last. Be sure to include:
   a. Brief description of the business. Include your mission statement.
   b. Brief overview of the market for your product.
   c. Brief overview of the strategic actions you plan to take to make your company a success.
   d. Brief overview of the managerial and technical experience and expertise of the key people.
   e. Brief statement of what the financial needs are and what would the money be used for. In addition, income statements and balance sheets for the last three years of operation if you are not a new business.

2.0 Company Summary

   a. Company Background
      Provide a brief background of your business. If your business is new, tell how you came up with the idea and how you got started. For an existing business, give a brief history with milestones and current situation.
   b. The Business
      What makes your business unique? How does it create value for your customers? Describe the key factors that will dictate the success of your business (i.e. price competitiveness, quality, durability, dependability, technical features, etc.)
   c. The Vision

3.0 Market Analysis Summary

   1. Include demographics about the potential buyers of your product/service.
   2. What is their motivation to buy?
   3. How many customers does the market contain? (How large is the market?)
   4. What are their potential annual purchases?
   5. What is the nature of the buying cycle?
      a. Is this product a durable good that lasts for years or a product that is repurchased on a regular basis?
      b. Is this product likely to be purchased at only seasonal periods during the year?

   3.1 Specific Target Market
      What do we know about the potential customer we are likely to sell to in our geographic area?
      1. If yours is a consumer product:
         a. What are the product features which you feel influences the consumer's buying decision?
         b. What, if any, research supports your feeling?
         c. Does the consumer have a preference in where he/she purchases comparable products? How strong is this preference?

3.2 Break-even Analysis
      a. What volume of inventory do you need to sell at what price to break-even?
      b. Why and how did you set prices? Four main elements of pricing: (1) material and supplies, (2) labor and operating expenses, (3) planned profit and (4) competition.

3.3 External Market Influence
How might each of the following external factors affect the sale or profitability of your product?
    1. Economic Factors such as:
        a. Inflation
        b. Recession
        c. High or low unemployment
    2. Social Factors such as:
        a. Age of customers
        b. Locational demographics
        c. Income levels
        d. Size of household
        e. Specific societal attitudes

3.4 Competitor Analysis
Describe each of the following factors and discuss how these factors will influence your success.
    1. Existing Competitors
        a. Who are they? List major known competitors.
        b. Why do you believe the potential customers in your target market buy from them now?
    2. Potential companies who might enter the market
        a. Who are they and when and why might they enter the market?
        b. What would be the impact in your target market segment if they enter?
    3. What are the strengths and weaknesses of each competitor's business?

4.0 Strategic and Implementation Plan

    1. How do you plan to market your products to the target market you identified above? Please specify your marketing strategy on key factors such as:
      a. Pricing
      b. Product promotion and advertising
      c. Customer services
    2. How will your products match up against those presently in the market? Compare on a competitor by competitor basis?

5.0 Management Summary

    1. How is your business organized?
      a. Legally (sole proprietorship, partnership, corporation, S corporation)
      b. Functionally
    2. Who are the key people (or will be) in your business? What are their backgrounds and what do they bring to the business that will enhance the chance of its success?

BUSINESS PLAN OUTLINE ●●●●●●●

6.0 Financial Plan

1. How much money do you need to make this product and your business a long-term success?
   a. Tie the response to this question to your production and marketing plan.
   b. Be realistic and specific.
2. Prepare a cash budget. Show the banker or investor what you need in terms of money, when you need it, and how and when you plan to generate revenues from operations and sales.
3. Have a realistic projection of costs of operations.
   a. Materials and supplies
   b. Labor
   c. Equipment
   d. Marketing
   e. Overhead
   f. Other (i.e. unique start-up costs)
4. Present balance sheets and income statements (projection) for the first three years of operation.

7.0 Strategic Action Plan

1. Clear mission statement for your business.
2. Specific performance goals and objectives.
3. Restatement of your production and marketing strategies.
4. How these strategies will be converted into operating action plans.
5. What control procedures do you plan to establish to keep the business on track?

8.0 Appendix

1. Tax Returns of principals for the last 3 years
2. Personal Financial Statement
3. Franchised Business - Copy of franchise contract and all supporting documents provided by the franchisor
4. Copy of proposed lease or purchase agreement for building space
5. Copy of resumes or curriculum vitae of all principals
6. Letters of reference for principle people
7. Copies of letters of intent from suppliers

Revised 05/ 27/ 2003
Outline courtesy of Dr. Tom Zimmerer, Clemson University Emerging Technology Center (1988)

Cover Sheet

_____

Company Name

_____   _____

Name of Principle People   Title

_____   _____

Name of Principle People   Title

_____   _____

Name of Principle People   Title

_____

Street Address

_____   _____   _____

City   State   Zip Code

_____

Phone Number

_____

Fax Number

_____

Email Address

_____

Web Address

Confidentiality Agreement

The undersigned reader acknowledges that the information provided by _____ in this business plan is confidential; therefore, reader agrees not to disclose it without the express written permission of _____ DBA _____.

It is acknowledged by reader that information to be furnished in this business plan is in all respects confidential in nature, other than information which is in the public domain through other means and that any disclosure or use of same by the reader, may cause serious harm or damage to _____.

Upon request, this document is to be immediately returned to _____.

_____
Signature

_____
Name (printed or typed)

_____
Date

This is a business plan. It does not imply an offering of securities.

Table of Contents

Business Plan

1.0 Executive Summary

The executive summary should not exceed two typewritten pages. The executive summary should encapsulate your entire plan with emphasis on major highlights to peak your reader's attention and $$$. Therefore, it is best to write it last. Be sure to include:

1. Brief description of the business. Include your mission statement.
2. Brief overview of the market for your product.
3. Brief overview of the strategic actions you plan to take to make your company a success.
4. Brief overview of the managerial and technical experience and expertise of the key people.
5. Brief statement of what the financial needs are and what would the money be used for. In addition, income statements and balance sheets for the last three years of operation if you are not a new business.

_____

_____

_____

_____

_____

_____

_____

_____

_____

_____

_____

_____

_____

_____

_____

_____

2.0 Company Summary

a. Company Background

Provide a brief background of your business. If your business in new, tell how you came up with the idea and how you got started. For an existing business, give a brief history with milestones and current situation.

b. The Business

What makes your business unique? How does it create value for your customers? Describe the key factors that will dictate the success of your business (i.e. price competitiveness, quality, durability, dependability, technical features, etc.)

c. The Vision

_____

_____

_____

_____

_____

_____

_____

_____

_____

_____

_____

_____

_____

_____

_____

_____

_____

_____

_____

3.0 Market Analysis Summary

1. Include demographics about the potential buyers of your product/service.
2. What is their motivation to buy?
3. How many customers does the market contain? (How large is the market?)
4. What are their potential annual purchases?
5. What is the nature of the buying cycle?
   a. Is this product a durable good that lasts for years or a product that is repurchased on a regular basis?
   b. Is this product likely to be purchased at only seasonal periods during the year?

_____

_____

_____

_____

_____

_____

_____

_____

_____

_____

_____

_____

_____

_____

_____

_____

_____

_____

3.1 Specific Target Market

What do we know about the potential customer we are likely to sell to in our geographic area?
1. If yours is a consumer product:
    a. What are the product features, which you feel, influences the consumer's buying decision?
    b. What, if any, research supports your feeling?
    c. Does the consumer have a preference in where he/she purchases comparable products? How strong is this preference?

_____

_____

_____

_____

_____

_____

_____

_____

_____

_____

_____

_____

_____

_____

_____

_____

_____

_____

_____

_____

3.2 Break-even Analysis

    a.   What volume of inventory do you need to sell at what price to break-even?

    b.   Why and how did you set prices? Four main elements of pricing: (1) material and supplies, (2) labor and operating expenses, (3) planned profit and (4) competition.

_____

_____

_____

_____

_____

_____

_____

_____

_____

_____

_____

_____

You can include a graph

3.3 External Market Influence

How might each of the following external factors affect the sale or profitability of your product?

1. Economic Factors such as:
   a. Inflation
   b. Recession
   c. High or low unemployment
2. Social Factors such as:
   a. Age of customers
   b. Locational demographics
   c. Income levels
   d. Size of household
   e. Specific societal attitudes

_____

_____

_____

_____

_____

_____

_____

_____

_____

_____

_____

_____

_____

_____

_____

_____

_____

_____

3.4 Competitor Analysis

Describe each of the following factors and discuss how these factors will influence your success.
1. Existing Competitors
   a. Who are they? List major known competitors.
   b. Why do you believe the potential customers in your target market buy from them now?
2. Potential companies who might enter the market
   a. Who are they and when and why might they enter the market?
   b. What would be the impact in your target market segment if they enter?
3. What are the strengths and weaknesses of each competitor's business?

_____

_____

_____

_____

_____

_____

_____

_____

_____

_____

_____

_____

_____

_____

_____

_____

_____

_____

4.0 Strategic and Implementation Plan

1. How do you plan to market your products to the target market you identified above? Please specify your marketing strategy on key factors such as:
   a. Pricing
   b. Product promotion and advertising
   c. Customer services
2. How will your products match up against those presently in the market? Compare on a competitor-by-competitor basis?

5.0 Management Summary

1. How is your business organized?
   a. Legally (sole proprietorship, partnership, corporation, S corporation)
   b. Functionally
2. Who are the key people (or will be) in your business? What are their backgrounds and what do they bring to the business that will enhance the chance of its success?

6.0 Financial Plan

1. How much money do you need to make this product and your business a long-term success?
   a. Tie the response to this question to your production and marketing plan. Be realistic and specific.
2. Prepare a cash budget. Show the banker or investor what you need in terms of money, when you need it, and how and when you plan to generate revenues from operations and sales.
3. Have a realistic projection of costs of operations.
   a. Materials and supplies
   b. Labor
   c. Equipment
   d. Marketing
   e. Overhead
   f. Other (i.e. unique start-up costs)
4. Present balance sheets and income statements (projection) for the first three years of operation.

BUSINESS PLAN NARRATIVE ●●●●●●●

6.1 Initial Cash Requirments for a New Business and Budget

These are general expenses typically incurred during start-up and monthly operation. Tailor this form to fit the requirements of your business.

START-UP DOLLARS NEEDED

Expense	Amount	Description
Advertising	_____	Promotion for opening the business
Beginning Inventory	_____	Amount of inventory needed to open
Building construction	_____	Amount per contractor bid and other
Cash	_____	Requirements for the cash register
Decorating	_____	Estimate based on bid if applicable
Deposits	_____	Check with utility companies
Fixtures and Equipment	_____	Use actual bid on all fixtures and equipment
Installing fixtures and Equipment	_____	Use actual bids and other
Insurance	_____	Bid from insurance agent
Lease Payment	_____	Amount to be paid before opening
Licenses and Permits	_____	Check with city or state officials
Miscellaneous	_____	All other
Professional Fees	_____	Include business mentor, accountant, attorney, engineer, etc.
Remodeling	_____	Amount per contractor bid and other
Rent	_____	Amount to be paid before opening
Services	_____	Cleaning, accounting, etc.
Signs	_____	Amount per contractor bid and other
Supplies	_____	Office, cleaning, etc
Unanticipated Expenses	_____	Include a reasonable amount for the unexpected
Other	_____	
Other	_____	
Other	_____	

TOTAL START-UP DOLLARS $ _____ Total amount of costs before opening

REPEATING MONTHLY EXPENSES

In the repeating monthly expense include the first three months cash needs unless otherwise noted.

Expense	Amount	Description
Advertising		
Bank Service Charges	_____	
Credit Card Fees	_____	
Delivery Charges	_____	
Donations/Charitable Giving	_____	
Dues and Subscriptions	_____	
Health Insurance	_____	Not including the amount included above
Insurance	_____	Not including the amount included above
Interest	_____	
Inventory	_____	*** See description below
Lease Payments	_____	Not including the amount included above
Loan Payments	_____	Principal and interest payments
Miscellaneous	_____	
Office Expenses	_____	
Payroll other than owner or manager	_____	
Payroll Taxes	_____	
Professional Fees	_____	
Rent	_____	Not including the amount included above
Repairs and Maintenance	_____	
Salary of Owner and Manager	_____	Include only if applicable for three months
Sales Tax	_____	
Supplies	_____	
Telephone	_____	
Utilities	_____	
Other	_____	
Other	_____	
Other	_____	*** Include the amount that will be needed to expand your inventory. If inventory is to be replaced from cash sales do not include here. Assume the sale generated sufficient cash for the replacement.

TOTAL REPEATING EXPENSES $ _____

TOTAL CASH NEEDED AT START-UP $ _____

BUSINESS PLAN NARRATIVE ●●●●●●

6.2 Profit Loss (Income) Statement

	JAN	FEB	MAR	APR	MAY	JUN	JUL	AUG	SEP	OCT	NOV	DEC
INCOME												
Gross Sales												
Less returns												
Less Discounts												
Less Debts												
Interest, Rent, Royalties												
Total Income												
EXPENSES												
Cost of Goods Sold												
Direct Payroll												
Indirect Payroll												
Taxes other than income tax												
Sales Expenses												
Postage and Shipping												
Advertising and Promotion												
Office Expenses												
Travel and Entertainment												
Phone												
Other Utilities												
Automobile												
Insurance												
Professional Fees												
Rent												
Interest on Loans												
Other, Miscellaneous												
Total Expenses												
Net Income												
Less Income Taxes												
NET INCOME AFTER TAXES												

BUSINESS PLAN NARRATIVE ●●●●●

6.3 Balance Sheet

ASSETS	Start	JAN	FEB	MAR	APR	MAY	JUN	JUL	AUG	SEP	OCT	NOV	DEC
Current Assets													
Cash Balance													
Accounts Receivable													
Inventory													
Other Current Assets													
Subtotal													
Capital Assets													
Accumulated Depreciation													
Subtotal													
Total Assets													
LIABILITIES													
Current Liabilities													
Accounts Payable													
Current Notes													
Other Current Liabilities													
Subtotal													
Long-term Liabilities													
Total Liabilities													
CAPITAL													
Paid-in Capital													
Retained Earnings													
Earnings													
Total Capital													
Total Capital and Liabilities													
NET WORTH													

7.0 Strategic Action Plan

1. Clear mission statement for your business.
2. Specific performance goals and objectives.
3. Restatement of your production and marketing strategies.
4. How these strategies will be converted into operating action plans.
5. What control procedures do you plan to establish to keep the business on track?

8.0 Appendix

1. Tax Returns of principals for the last 3 years
2. Personal Financial Statement
3. Franchised Business - Copy of franchise contract and all supporting documents provided by the franchisor
4. Copy of proposed lease or purchase agreement for building space
5. Copy of resumes or curriculum vitae of all principals
6. Letters of reference for principle people
7. Copies of letters of intent from suppliers

§ Attach these documents and/or other documents applicable to/requested for your business plan proposal.

Revised 05/ 27/ 2003
Outline courtesy of Dr. Tom Zimmerer, Clemson University Emerging Technology Center (1988)

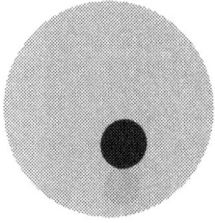

COMMUNICATING THE VISION

"Who is a wise man and endued with knowledge among you? Let him shew out of good conversation his works with meekness of wisdom."
James 3:13 KJV

MARKETING YOUR BUSINESS ●●●●●●

Use the following worksheets to define and examine your market, develop a strategy to reach the people that demand your product/service, evaluate your current marketing program and create or revise your marketing plan.

Your Positioning Statement/Motto:

Your Strengths		*Your Customers Value*	
Explicit – can be expressed and stated	*Implicit – can only be experienced; not directly stated*		

Your Attributes *Adjectives that ascribe a quality about your company*	*Your Differentiation* *State the difference between you and others;* *Try to capture a difference that you "own"*

Your Target Market *Adapt the categories to information relevant to your target market*	
Descriptor	
Age	
Sex	
Socio Economic	
Race	

Brand Association *Reputable companies that are tied to your product and/or service i.e. - Microsoft Certified Computer Dealer*	

MARKETING YOUR BUSINESS ●●●●●●

Your Message:

What do you want to tell people about you? The message should be relevant to them.

Media:

Where are they most likely to receive the message? These forms of media are not for every business. Invest in media that will give you access to your specific market that is effective according to your budget and advertising goals.

Media	In Use	Note
AM Radio	☐	
FM Radio	☐	
Television	☐	
Billboard	☐	
Phonebook	☐	
Website	☐	
Newspaper	☐	
Local Journals	☐	
Flyers/Postcards	☐	
Direct Mail	☐	
Promotional Items	☐	
Joint Marketing	☐	
	☐	
	☐	

To Do		
Complete	Who's Responsible	Task
☐		
☐		
☐		
☐		
☐		
☐		
☐		
☐		
☐		
☐		
☐		
☐		
☐		
☐		
☐		

Four Keys to Effective Marketing

① *Know Your Audience*

What are we currently known for in the market?

_____

_____

_____

What is the perception I'd like the market to have about my company?

_____

_____

_____

What is my mission? And how is it being communicated to my team (employees and partners)?

_____

_____

_____

The mission is being communicated through:

_____   _____

_____   _____

_____   _____

Does my identity connect with the market I am trying to reach? How does it and how does it not?

_____

_____

Source: *Your Church Magazine*, "Four Keys to Effective Church Outreach" by Scott Evans, May/June 2002

MARKETING YOUR BUSINESS ●●●●●●●

② Know Your Market

Where/Location	Interest/Attitudes	Age	Family Size	Income	Ethnicity	Needs	Hopes	Fears

*Make this analysis applicable to your market by adding and deleting categories. The goal is to gather relevant information that will help you plan, communicate, and reach your market more effectively and efficiently.

Source: *Your Church Magazine,* "Four Keys to Effective Church Outreach" by Scott Evans, May/June 2002

③ *Close the "Back Door" (Customer Retention/Repeat Customers)*

Do I offer incentives that make customers want to come back? If so, what?

_____

_____

Do I have an established strategy to move first time or one time customers to repeat customers? If so, what?

_____

_____

Is there a culture of acceptance and connection to potential repeat customers?

_____

_____

Do my employees understand that it is their responsibility not just to be friendly, but also to build relationships with new customers?

_____

_____

④ *Make Marketing Easy*

Is my team equipped with the attitude and aptitude to draw in and retain new customers? If so, how?

_____

_____

_____

_____

Source: *Your Church Magazine*, "Four Keys to Effective Church Outreach" by Scott Evans, May/June 2002

Penetrating and Expanding Your Market and Profitability:
How to Market Your Product to a Retailer

1. *Market Research*
   First, know your market:
   - ✓ Who - who you sell your product to, their demographic information
   - ✓ When - their buying patterns
   - ✓ Why - why will they buy your product - quality, incentives, likes/dislikes, needs
   - ✓ How - how you will reach them – your message, types of advertising, location

2. *Develop a Sales Strategy*
   Once you have attracted the customer, sales strategy is how you will close the deal. In the case of selling to a retail store, they ultimately attract the consumer so your challenge is:
   - ✓ How will you get the retailer to buy or stock your product?
   - ✓ Evaluate if the retailer has the ability to attract and close a sell with the people who will buy your product.
   - ✓ Will the retailer's image and advertising attract the type of people who will buy your product?

3. *Find local retail stores who can add your product to their product lines.*

4. *Visit the Stores as a Consumer*
   - ✓ Scope out the store, the sales people, type of products sold, and the customers in the store buying. Do you think this retailer will make a good partnership?
   - ✓ Try to meet the owner/manager (decision maker) on an informal level. If you can't meet them at that time, get their name and number and come back.
   - ✓ Buy something!

5. *Contact the Decision Maker*
   - ✓ If the decision maker is accessible in the store, approach them with your proposition. If not, make a phone call.
   - ✓ Take 90 seconds to introduce yourself and your product. Mention bits and pieces to peak their interest so they'll give you an appointment or more time.
   - ✓ Mention measurable outcomes of the partnership, such as #'s, $$$, statistics, benefits!!!

6. *At Your Appointment:*
   - ✓ Take samples (targeted samples, if applicable). It may benefit you to LEAVE a sample aka "a gift".
   - ✓ A proposal with company information, a price quote, revenue potential and other retail store references.
   - ✓ Be enthusiastic, be real, be genuine, be interested, be confident, be PREPARED and be ON-TIME!

8. *Last but first, consult Bernell to help you get prepared to close the deal!*

③ *Close the "Back Door" (Customer Retention/Repeat Customers)*

Do I offer incentives that make customers want to come back? If so, what?

_____

_____

Do I have an established strategy to move first time or one time customers to repeat customers? If so, what?

_____

_____

Is there a culture of acceptance and connection to potential repeat customers?

_____

_____

Do my employees understand that it is their responsibility not just to be friendly, but also to build relationships with new customers?

_____

_____

④ *Make Marketing Easy*

Is my team equipped with the attitude and aptitude to draw in and retain new customers? If so, how?

_____

_____

_____

_____

Source: *Your Church Magazine*, "Four Keys to Effective Church Outreach" by Scott Evans, May/June 2002

Penetrating and Expanding Your Market and Profitability:
How to Market Your Product to a Retailer

1. *Market Research*
   First, know your market:
   - ✓ Who - who you sell your product to, their demographic information
   - ✓ When - their buying patterns
   - ✓ Why - why will they buy your product - quality, incentives, likes/dislikes, needs
   - ✓ How - how you will reach them – your message, types of advertising, location

2. *Develop a Sales Strategy*
   Once you have attracted the customer, sales strategy is how you will close the deal. In the case of selling to a retail store, they ultimately attract the consumer so your challenge is:
   - ✓ How will you get the retailer to buy or stock your product?
   - ✓ Evaluate if the retailer has the ability to attract and close a sell with the people who will buy your product.
   - ✓ Will the retailer's image and advertising attract the type of people who will buy your product?

3. *Find local retail stores who can add your product to their product lines.*

4. *Visit the Stores as a Consumer*
   - ✓ Scope out the store, the sales people, type of products sold, and the customers in the store buying. Do you think this retailer will make a good partnership?
   - ✓ Try to meet the owner/manager (decision maker) on an informal level. If you can't meet them at that time, get their name and number and come back.
   - ✓ Buy something!

5. *Contact the Decision Maker*
   - ✓ If the decision maker is accessible in the store, approach them with your proposition. If not, make a phone call.
   - ✓ Take 90 seconds to introduce yourself and your product. Mention bits and pieces to peak their interest so they'll give you an appointment or more time.
   - ✓ Mention measurable outcomes of the partnership, such as #'s, $$$, statistics, benefits!!!

6. *At Your Appointment:*
   - ✓ Take samples (targeted samples, if applicable). It may benefit you to LEAVE a sample aka "a gift".
   - ✓ A proposal with company information, a price quote, revenue potential and other retail store references.
   - ✓ Be enthusiastic, be real, be genuine, be interested, be confident, be PREPARED and be ON-TIME!

8. *Last but first, consult Bernell to help you get prepared to close the deal!*

PRACTICAL EVERYDAY MARKETING IDEAS

One goal of marketing is to get your name out as often, and keep your name out as often and as inexpensively as possible. Grab some of these practical ideas that you can use to market your business in everyday life.

Grab Ideas

- Carry a camera with you to take a shot of items that help you generate ideas. A picture is worth a thousand words when you are trying to remember or explain a concept.
- Attend trade shows of other services, i.e., if you are into apparel, go to a foods trade show. Think outside of the box. There may be ideas you can gain because this area is so different from yours.

Image

- Develop a style or trademark that is all your own. When people think of you, they can think of that special feature about you and your business.
- Use a consistent logo, theme, and picture on all your correspondence – envelopes, note cards, business cards, invoices, thank you notes, etc.
- Choose a signature color/theme for you business and wear a uniform. When people see you, they will know you are a professional in your field.
- Wear a nametag.
- Place your sticker, logo, or emblem on all your outgoing mail.
- Make your product memorable and appealing to people of all ages, races, etc.
- Make sure that you and your entire staff get all the medical shots needed for your area of business. Use this as a way to tell potential customers, especially if you are in food service and healthcare, that your business is a safe place.

Service and Attitude Is Linked Directly to You

- Be fair and honest, and be motivated to be a star performer throughout your career.
- Strive to act like/talk like and be the most knowledgeable person in your field or area of business expertise.
- Be generous.
- Aim for contracts of all sizes. Let no one be too insignificant for your service.
- Never become so busy doing your work that you are not able to think about how you are doing your work.
- THINK BIG!!!
- Be genuinely interested in others.
- Write and mail handwritten thank you notes.
- Be flexible and creative.

PRACTICAL EVERYDAY MARKETING IDEAS ●●●●●●●

Getting Your Name Out

- Focus on doing what matters MOST to keep your business visible and positive.
- Place a stack of your business cards, brochures, book, or portfolio every place that welcomes them (professional offices such as medical, dental, and accountant's offices, restaurants, etc.)
- Attend grand openings of other businesses. NEWTORK! NETWORK! NETWORK!
- Make sure you are well known in the community. You want to be the first person contacted when there is a need for your product or services.
- Host an open house once each year. Most businesses do this at holiday/Christmas time. Choose a time when there is not as much activity going on in people's lives.
- Join with other businesses to co-host a sidewalk or driveway sale. You can get rid of overstock and/or buy low priced stock for this special event.
- Leave your business card when you give a generous tip at restaurants. This is not a good idea if you are not generous in your tipping.
- Ask customers for referrals: Remember birds of a feather flock together. Only ask those customers who represent the type of client you want to have.
- Phone in to radio talk shows and identify yourself.
- Go to free functions – concerts, plays, museums, etc. There are many opportunities for networking.
- Tour open houses for sale or under construction and leave your business card.
- Put an insert/ad/announcement or insert in your church bulletin.
- Post a note/business cards at local grocery stores, churches, markets, public bulletin boards, college campuses, the YMCA, convenience stores, your area community center, the library or any other place that allows such notices to be placed.
- Go to flea markets to network.
- Go to business functions that occur when you join the Chamber of Commerce and/or Better Business Bureaus; exchange business cards. Send handwritten follow-up notes to the people you meet.
- Volunteer once per month at a school, recreation center or local school sports function; pass out your cards or flyers.

Communicating Your Price & Managing Finances

- Give written quotes and estimates whenever possible; add the note: "prices are subject to change without notice."
- Always send invoices promptly.
- Know your banker. Contact him/her frequently and make sure you are utilizing all services available to your business.

The Key Is People

- Surround yourself with people/teammates who do well what you do not do well.
- Give your staff bonuses for business that they generate.

PRACTICAL EVERYDAY MARKETING IDEAS ●●●●●●●

The Key Is People (continued)

- MENTOR at least one person who may be interested in your line of work.
- Utilize experts in areas where needed. Pick his/her brain and write down all your ideas.
- Spend time with your mentor.

Don't Only Say It, Show It

- Use a camera to record before, during, and after shots of your work. Let your work speak for itself.
- Seek to always have samples of your product and/or small thank you gifts.
- Put a sign on your work or label your products. Notice how contractors/builders and architects label the area in front of the job site.
- Have a yearly raffle of a giant basket of goodies. This could be a joint effort for you and other businesses.

Professional Development/Be In the Know

- Commit to lifelong learning and taking continuing education classes.
- Send a note/letter to all magazines in your trade area and request a sample copy. This will put you on various mailing lists.

Be Prepared

- Always have an updated resume ready to mail out when opportunity comes your way.

Logistics

- Use a P.O. Box for billing and a street address for personal correspondence.
- Put a magnetic sign on your vehicle.

Have You Thought About This

- Allow children to have access to your resources.
- Write all of your favorite actors/actresses and request-autographed photos. Add these to your portfolio.
- Think: A card a day keeps the rent paid.
- Send birthday cards to children – future clients.
- Teach a class. Local technical colleges welcome individuals to enhance their continuing education offerings.

Originally drafted by Debra A. King-Johnson, PhD, LPC, Family C.A.R.E. Services, Seneca, SC 2000
Updated and revised by Bernell L. King, Visions International, 2002

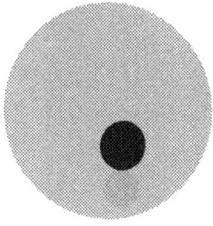

FINANCING THE VISION

"For which of you, intending to build a tower, does not sit down first and count the cost, whether he has enough to finish it..."
Luke 14:28

SAMPLE MONTHLY BUDGET SHEET ●●●●●●

MONTHLY INCOME AND EXPENSES

| | | MONTH OF | Jan-03 |

INCOME PER MONTH	Male	Female
Salary 1	2300	1900
Salary 2	0	0
Interests/Dividends	0	0
Child Support	0	0
Notes	0	0
Rental Income	0	0
Other	0	0
TOTAL GROSS INCOME	2300.00	1900.00
(1) Less Taxes & Social Security	345	285
NET INCOME	1955.00	1615.00
(2) Less Tithes & Offerings	300	250
COMBINED NET SPENDABLE INC	3020.00	

(3) HOUSING	Budget	Actual
Mortgage/Rent	650	650
Insurance (Homeowners/renters)	0	0
Taxes (If not included in mortgage)	0	0
Electricity	95	98
Gas	0	0
Water	0	0
Sanitation	0	0
Telephone	40	38
Maintenance	0	0
Security System	0	0
SUB TOTAL	785.00	786.00

(4) FOOD		
Grocery	150	165
Lunches	0	15
Other	0	0
SUB TOTAL	150.00	180.00

(5) TRANSPORTATION		
Auto Payments	320	320
Gas & Oil	80	72
Insurance*	40	40
License Fees	0	0
Taxes*	5	5
Public Transit (i.e. Bus, Taxi)	0	0
Maint./Repair/Replacement*	10	10
SUB TOTAL	455.00	447.00

(6) INSURANCE		
Life	35	35
Medical (Health)	15	15
Dental	5	5
Disability	0	0
Other	0	0
SUB TOTAL	55.00	55.00

(7) CHILD CARE	240.00	240.00

(8) DEBTS	Budget	Actual
Credit Card 1 (1456.00)	100	150
Credit Card 2 ( )	0	0
Child Support	0	0
Loans & Notes	50	50
2nd Mortgage	0	0
Other	0	0
SUB TOTAL	150.00	200.00

(9) ENTERTAINMENT/REC.		
Eating Out	50	70
Trips (weekend)	0	0
Babysitters	25	25
Activities (golf, tennis)	35	30
Vacation*	40	40
Other	0	0
SUB TOTAL	150.00	165.00

(10) CLOTHING	60.00	75.00

(11) SAVINGS	500.00	500.00

(12) MEDICAL *		
Doctor	25	25
Dentist	25	25
Medicine	25	25
Other	0	0
SUB TOTAL	75.00	75.00

(13) MISCELLANEOUS		
Toiletry, cosmetics	50	65
Beauty, barber	45	45
Laundry, dry cleaning	0	0
Allowances (children)	0	0
Subscriptions	0	0
Gifts (Christmas)*	10	10
Special Edu. & Tuition	0	0
Pocket Change Allow.		
(You and Spouse)	0	0
Cable	50	50
Internet Service	10	15
Other	0	0
SUB TOTAL	165.00	185.00

(14) TOTAL EXPENSES	2785.00	2908.00

INCOME VS. EXPENSES

(15) NET SPENDABLE INC	$3,020.00	$3,020.00
(16) LESS EXPENSES	$2,785.00	$2,908.00
(17) DIFFERENCE + or -	$235.00	$112.00

*Put in savings account until ready to be used

48

PERSONAL MONTHLY BUDGET ●●●●●●

MONTH OF _____

INCOME PER MONTH	Male	Female
Salary 1		
Salary 2		
Interests/Dividends		
Child Support		
Notes		
Rental Income		
Other		
TOTAL GROSS INCOME		
(1) Less Taxes & Social Security		
NET INCOME		
(2) Less Tithes & Offerings		
COMBINED NET SPENDABLE INC		

(3) HOUSING	Budget	Actual
Mortgage/Rent		
Insurance (Homeowners/renters)		
Taxes (If not included in mortgage)		
Electricity		
Gas		
Water		
Sanitation		
Telephone		
Maintenance		
Security System		
Other		
SUB TOTAL		

(4) FOOD		
Grocery		
Lunches		
Other		
SUB TOTAL		

(5) TRANSPORTATION		
Auto Payments		
Gas & Oil		
Insurance*		
License Fees		
Taxes*		
Public Transit (i.e. Bus, Taxi)		
Maint./Repair/Replacement*		
SUB TOTAL		

(6) INSURANCE		
Life		
Medical (Health)		
Dental		
Disability		
Other		
SUB TOTAL		

(7) CHILD CARE

(8) DEBTS	Budget	Actual
Credit Card 1 ( )		
Credit Card 2 ( )		
Child Support		
Loans & Notes		
2nd Mortgage		
Other		
SUB TOTAL		

(9) ENTERTAINMENT/REC.		
Eating Out		
Trips (weekend)		
Babysitters		
Activities (golf, tennis)		
Vacation*		
Other		
SUB TOTAL		

(10) CLOTHING

(11) SAVINGS

(12) MEDICAL *		
Doctor		
Dentist		
Medicine		
Other		
SUB TOTAL		

(13) MISCELLANEOUS		
Toiletry, cosmetics		
Beauty, barber		
Laundry, dry cleaning		
Allowances (children)		
Subscriptions		
Gifts (Christmas)*		
Special Edu. & Tuition		
Pocket Change Allow.		
(You and Spouse)		
Cable/Satellite		
Internet Service		
Mobile Phone		
Other		
SUB TOTAL		

(14) TOTAL EXPENSES

INCOME VS. EXPENSES

(15) NET SPENDABLE INC

(16) LESS EXPENSES

(17) DIFFERENCE + or -

*Put in savings account until ready to be used

49

PERSONAL MONTHLY BUDGET

	Jan	Feb	Mar	Apr	May	Jun	Jul	Aug	Sep	Oct	Nov	Dec	Total
Income:													
Wages (take-home) - partner 1													
Wages (take-home) - partner 2													
Interest and dividends													
Other													
Total Income													
Expenses:													
Auto expenses													
Auto insurance													
Auto payment													
Beauty shop and barber													
Cable TV													
Charity													
Child Care													
Clothing													
Credit card payments													
Dues and subscriptions													
Entertainment and recreation													
Gifts													
Groceries and dining out													
Health insurance													
Home repairs													
Household													
Income tax (additional)													
Laundry and dry cleaning													
Life insurance													
Medical and dental													
Mortgage payment or rent													
Other debt payments													
Telephone bill													
Tuition													
Utilities													
Vacations													
Other													
Total Expenses													

Source: Entrepreneur.com

50

MANAGING YOUR PERSONAL CREDIT ●●●●●●

What is a Credit Report?

There are three leading credit reporting agencies in the United States – Equifax, Transunion and Experian. Each maintains information about you and your credit history. This information is gathered on an ongoing basis from many sources that have extended you credit.

Lenders, employers, landlords, and other service providers buy that information in the form of a credit report to help them decide whether to approve your application for a loan, credit card, job, or housing, or to offer you a product or service at a particular rate.

Because your credit file changes constantly, it's important that you review your information regularly to check its accuracy. Do you need to check yours now?

What Information is Included?

Personal information. Compiled from credit applications you've filled out, this information normally includes your name, current and recent addresses, Social Security Number, date of birth, and current and previous employers.

Credit history. The bulk of your credit report consists of details about credit accounts that were opened in your name or that list you as an authorized user (such as a spouse's credit card). Account details, which are supplied by creditors with which you have an account, include the date the account was opened, the credit limit or amount of the loan, the payment terms, the balance, and a history that shows whether or not you've paid the account on time. Closed or inactive accounts, depending on the manner in which they were paid, stay on your report for 7 to 11 years from the date of their last activity.

Inquiries. Credit reporting agencies record an inquiry whenever your credit report is shown to another party, such as a lender, service provider, landlord, or insurer. Inquiries remain on your credit report for up to two years.

Public records. Matters of public record obtained from government sources such as courts of law -- including liens, bankruptcies, and overdue child support -- may appear on your credit report. Most public record information stays on your credit report for 7 years.

What is Not Included?

A credit report does not include information about your checking or savings accounts, bankruptcies that are more than 10 years old, charged-off or debts placed for collection that are more than seven years old, gender, ethnicity, religion, political affiliation, medical history, or criminal records. Your credit score is generated by information on your credit report, but is not part of the report itself.

Who Can Look at Your Credit Report?

Anyone with what is considered a permissible purpose can look at your report. These companies, groups, and individuals include:
- Potential lenders
- Landlords
- Insurance companies
- Employers and potential employers (usually only with your written consent)
- Companies you allow to monitor your account for signs of identity theft
- Some groups considering your application for a government license or benefit
- A state or local child support enforcement agency
- Any government agency (although they may be allowed to view only certain portions)
- Someone who uses your credit report to provide a product or service you have requested
- Someone that has your written authorization to obtain your credit report

Checking Your Report

Your credit report is used by many different lenders and other entities to make decisions about you. When it comes to your credit report, it's **what you don't know that can hurt you.** Credit card companies, mortgage loan companies, auto loan and insurance companies, even landlords and employers check credit reports to find out about your credit past. The reason? They figure if you were responsible in the past, you will most likely be responsible in the future.

When it's time to consider any sort of financial move -- a new home or car, a new credit card, a new auto insurance policy, even a new job -- it's time to check your report.

After You Get Your Report

When you get your report, review it carefully. If you see problems on your report, such as an unpaid bill that you simply forgot about, act right away to resolve the debt. Then ask the business to whom you owed the money to send a letter to the credit reporting agencies saying that the matter has been resolved.

Also, make sure your report is accurate. Check for accounts you didn't open, charges you didn't make, and delinquencies you didn't cause. If you see evidence of fraud, contact the credit reporting agencies immediately. Explain the situation and ask that a fraud alert be placed in your file. Also report the fraud to the police.

Your credit report will follow you throughout your life and can help you financially -- or hurt you. Review it carefully!

3-in-1 Credit Report are also available. It allows you to see your credit history as reported by the three major credit reporting agencies.

Source: www.equifax.com

MANAGING YOUR PERSONAL CREDIT ●●●●●●

To Receive Your Credit Report

Due to the rise in Identity Theft, you are now able to receive one (1) free credit report from each Credit Reporting Agency each year, effective June 1, 2005. To receive your free credit reports visit or call:
www.annualcreditreport.com
1.877.322.8228

❏   Equifax Credit Report
     1.800.685.1111
     Post Office Box 740241
     Atlanta, GA 30374
     www.equifax.com

❏   Experian Credit Report
     1.888.397.3742
     Post Office Box 2002
     Allen, TX 75013
     www.experian.com

❏   Transunion Credit Report
     1.800.888.4213
     Post Office Box 1000
     Chester, PA 19022
     www.transunion.com

Generally, by mail, the following basic information is required in writing with a signature:

- First Name, Middle Name, Last Name with Jr., Sr., II, or III, if applicable
- Spouse's First Name
- Current Address with apartment number
- Proof of current address by a copy of a utility bill, phone bill, driver's license, or bank statement
- Previous Addresses for last 5 years
- Social Security Number and copy of your card for verification
- Date of Birth
- Current Employer – Name and Address
- Home Phone Number
- Check or Money Order payable to respective credit reporting agency

*** Fees for reports vary by state (see following table) and each reporting agency may be require different information therefore, call the agency to verify you have all necessary information before you send your request. The fee for each credit report is typically $9.00 in the state of South Carolina. You can also receive your credit score for an extra fee.

MANAGING YOUR PERSONAL CREDIT ●●●●●●

To Receive Your Credit Report (continued)

By law, you are entitled to disclosure of your credit file. The charge is under $10.00 and may be reduced or free in some states. See below:

State	Free	Fee	Subsequent/Additional Requests
California		$ 8.00	
Colorado	1 per calendar year	$ 8.00	
Connecticut		$ 5.00	$ 7.50 with in 12 months
Georgia	2 per calendar	$ 9.00	
Maine	1 with in 12 months	$ 5.00	
Maryland	1 with in 12 months	$ 5.00	
Massachusetts	1 per calendar year	$ 8.00	
Minnesota		$ 3.00	$ 9.00 with in 12 months
Montana		$ 8.50	
New Jersey	1 with in 12 months	$ 8.00	
Vermont	1 with in 12 months	$ 7.50	
All other states		$ 9.00	
*Unemployed	1 with in 12 months		
*Welfare	1 with in 12 months		

You are entitled to one free report during any 12-month period no matter where you live, if you:

- Are unemployed and intend to apply for employment in the next 60 days
- Are on public welfare assistance
- Believe your file contains inaccurate information due to fraud
- You are also entitled to a free report if you have received notice of an adverse decision (such as denial of credit, insurance, or employment) within the past 60 days

To Obtain Your Credit Score

By law, you are entitled to obtain your credit score. To request your credit score, contact the respective credit reporting agencies. Each CRA has a different score, generally within the same range, and charge an additional fee. If you are in the process of obtaining a mortgage, you may be entitled to free credit score information. Contact the person making or arranging your loan for further information.

KNOW YOUR RIGHTS ●●●●●●

Summary Of Your Rights Under The Fair Credit Reporting Act

The federal Fair Credit Reporting Act (FCRA) is designed to promote accuracy, fairness, and privacy of information in the files of every "consumer reporting agency" (CRA). Most CRAs are credit bureaus that gather and sell information about you—such as if you pay your bills on time or have filed bankruptcy—to creditors, employers, landlords, and other businesses. You can find the complete text of the FCRA, 15 U.S.C. §§1681-1681, at the Federal Trade Commission's Web site (http://www.ftc.gov). The FCRA gives you specific rights, as outlined below. You may have additional rights under state law. You may contact a state or local consumer protection agency or a state attorney general to learn those rights.

Access to your file is limited. A CRA may provide information about you only to people with a need recognized by the FCRA—usually to consider an application with a creditor, insurer, employer, landlord, or other business.

Your consent is required for reports that are provided to employers, or reports that contain medical information. A CRA may not give out information about you to your employer, or prospective employer, without your written consent. A CRA may not report medical information about you to creditors, insurers, or employers without your permission. Written consent generally is not required in the trucking industry. For more information, go to www.ftc.gov/credit.

You can find out what is in your file. At your request, a CRA must give you the information in your file, and a list of everyone who has requested it recently. There is no charge for the report if a person has taken action against you because of information supplied by the CRA, if you request the report within 60 days of receiving notice of the action. You also are entitled to one free report every twelve months upon request if you certify that (1) adverse action has been taken against you because of information in your credit report (2) you are the victim of identify theft and place a fraud alert in your file (3) your file contains inaccurate information as a result of fraud (4) you are on public assistance (5) you are unemployed but expect to apply for employment within 60 days. Otherwise, a CRA may charge you a fee of up to nine dollars. **In addition, by September 2005 all consumers will be entitled to one free disclosure every 12 months upon request from each nationwide credit bureau and from nationwide specialty consumer reporting agencies. See www.ftc.gov/credit for additional information.**

You have the right to ask for a credit score. Credit scores are numerical summaries of your credit-worthiness based on information from credit bureaus. You may request a credit score from consumer reporting agencies that create scores or distribute scores used in residential real property loans, but you will have to pay for it. **In some mortgage transactions, you will receive credit score information for free from the mortgage lender.**

You must be told if information in your report has been used against you. Anyone who uses information from a CRA to take action against you—such as denying an application for credit, insurance, or employment—must tell you, and give you the name, address, and phone number of the CRA that provided the consumer report.

You can dispute incomplete or inaccurate information with the CRA. If you tell a CRA that your file contains inaccurate information, the CRA must reinvestigate the items (usually within 30 days) by presenting to its information source all relevant evidence you submit, unless your dispute is frivolous. The source must review your evidence and report its findings to the CRA. (The source also must advise national CRAs—to which it has provided the data—of any error.) The CRA must give you a written report of the investigation and a copy of the revisions made to your information if the investigation results in any change. If the CRA's investigation does not resolve the dispute, you may add a brief statement to your file. The CRA must normally include a summary of your dispute statement in future reports. If an item is deleted or a dispute statement is filed, you may ask that anyone who has recently received your report be notified of the change.

Inaccurate, incomplete, or unverifiable information must be corrected or deleted. A CRA must remove or correct inaccurate or unverified information from its files, usually within 30 days after you dispute it. **However, the CRA is not required to remove accurate data from your file unless it is outdated (as described later) or cannot be verified**. If your dispute results in any change to your report, the CRA cannot reinsert into your file a disputed item unless the information source verifies its accuracy and completeness. In addition, the CRA must give you a written notice telling you it has reinserted the item. The notice must include the name, address and phone number of the information source. **You can dispute inaccurate items with the source of the information**. If you tell anyone—such as a creditor who reports to a CRA—that you dispute an item, they may not then report the information to a CRA without including a notice of your dispute.

Outdated negative information may not be reported. In most cases, a CRA may not report negative information that is more than seven years old; ten years for bankruptcies.

You may choose to exclude your name from CRA lists for unsolicited credit and insurance offers. Creditors and insurers may use file information as the basis for sending you unsolicited offers of credit or insurance. Such offers must include a toll-free phone number for you to call if you want your name and address removed from future lists. If you call, you shall be kept off the lists for two years. The toll-free number for all of the national CRAs is 1 888 5OPTOUT (1 888 567 8688.) If you request, complete, and return the CRA from provided for this purpose, you shall be taken off the lists indefinitely.

You may seek damages from violators. If a CRA, a user or (in some cases) a provider of CRA data, violates the FCRA, you may sue them in state or federal court.

Identity theft victims and active duty military personnel have additional rights. For more information, visit www.ftc.gov/credit.

States may enforce the FCRA, and many states have their own consumer reporting laws. In some cases, you may have more rights under state law. For more information, contact your state or local consumer protection agency or your state Attorney General.

For Questions Or Concerns Regarding:	*Please Contact:*
CRAs, creditors and others not listed below	Federal Trade Commission – CRC 600 Pennsylvania Avenue, NW Washington, DC 20580 * 877 FTC HELP
Identity Theft	Identity Theft Data Clearinghouse 600 Pennsylvania Avenue, NW Washington, DC 20580 * 877 ID THEFT
National banks, federal branches/agencies of foreign banks (word "National" or initials "N.A." appear in or after bank's name)	Office of the Comptroller of the Currency Compliance Management, Mail Stop 6-6 Washington, DC 20219 * 800 613 6743
Federal Reserve System member banks (except national banks, and federal branches/agencies of foreign banks)	Federal Reserve Board Division of Consumer & Community Affairs Washington, DC 20551 * 202 452 3693
Savings associations and federally chartered savings banks (word "Federal" or initials "F.S.B." appear in federal institution's name)	Office of Thrift Supervision Consumer Programs Washington, DC 20552 * 800 842 6929
Federal credit unions (words "Federal Credit Union" appear in institution's name)	National Credit Union Administration 1775 Duke Street Alexandria, VA 22314 * 703 518 6360
State-chartered banks that are not members of the Federal Reserve System	Federal Deposit Insurance Corporation Division of Compliance & Consumer Affairs Washington, DC 20429 * 877 275 3342
Air, surface, or rail common carriers regulated by former Civil Aeronautics Board or Interstate Commerce Commission	Department of Transportation Office of Financial Management Washington, DC 20590 * 202 366 1306
Activities subject to the Packers and Stockyards Act, 1921	Department of Agriculture Office of Deputy Administrator – GIPSA Washington, DC 20250 * 202 720 7051

KNOW YOUR RIGHTS ●●●●●●

Fixing Errors on Your Report

It's possible for incorrect, incomplete or outdated information to appear on your credit report. If it does, it can drastically lower your chances of getting the loans, credit cards, and other credit products you deserve. If you find an error, take the following steps to fix it as soon as possible. If you see evidence of fraud, contact the credit reporting companies immediately. Explain the situation and ask that a fraud alert be placed in your file. Also report the fraud to the police, and your creditors.

Please note: It's important to keep a record of everything you do. Send all correspondence return receipt requested, and make copies of any letters or documents you send. Never send original documents. Also, document any and all phone/verbal contact with creditors with the date, time, and name (last name) or ID of the person you spoke with. Get a direct extension to this person, if available.

1. **Contact the Credit Reporting Company**

   Contact the credit reporting company that is reporting the item in question. You will need a printed copy of your credit report from them, which you may be eligible to receive free of charge.

   After you send written documentation of the inaccuracy, the credit reporting company will review it. If further investigation is required, they will provide notification of your dispute, including the relevant information you submitted, to the source that furnished the disputed information to them. The source will then review the information, conduct their own investigation, and report back. The credit reporting company will then make all appropriate changes to your credit file based on the investigation, and notify you of the update.

2. **Contact the Creditor Regarding the Problem**

   In some cases, you should contact the appropriate creditor or lender before contacting a credit reporting company. This is especially true if you are a victim of fraud. You should also contact the appropriate creditor or lender if that source has verified the information that you disputed with the credit reporting company. Most large creditors have standard procedures for customers to dispute items on their account. If you have proof that the item in question is incorrect, it should be resolved quickly.

   If the creditor finds that the disputed information is indeed incorrect, **the creditor is required under the Fair Credit Reporting Act to update its records both internally and with the credit reporting companies it deals with, usually within 30 days.** However, some small creditors that do not regularly report information to credit reporting companies are not required to notify the agencies of the corrected information. In these cases, you will need to contact the agency directly.

   Always follow up your phone calls with a letter. List each disputed item, and state how it is inaccurate, attaching copies of all relevant documents. Include your full name, account number, the dollar amount in question, and the reason you believe the item is wrong. Be concise.

3. **Contact the Other Credit Reporting Companies**

   If you find an inaccuracy with one credit bureau, you may want to get your credit report from the other two agencies to see if their reports contain the same error. After you've corrected an error with one agency, the other agencies will in most cases also receive the corrected information. But for prompt correction, it's best to contact each of the three major credit reporting companies yourself.

4. **Ensure the Error Is Fixed**

   Within 30 days (45 days if based upon your annual free credit file), the credit reporting company should notify you of the results of its investigation and provide you with a new credit report free of charge. Examine it carefully to ensure that the inaccuracies have been fixed or removed.

   If the error has been fixed, you can have the credit reporting company send the corrected report to anyone who received the inaccurate report in the past six months (two years in the case of employers).

5. **If You Cannot Resolve a Disputed Item**

   You have the right to file a brief statement with the consumer reporting agency, free of charge, explaining the nature of your disagreement. The consumer reporting agency may limit your statement to not more than 100 words if it provides you with assistance in writing a clear summary of the disagreement. Your statement will become part of your credit file, and will be included each time your credit file is accessed, for as long as the disputed item remains in your credit file.

PERSONAL FINANCIAL STATEMENT

U.S. SMALL BUSINESS ADMINISTRATION

As of _____ , _____

Complete this form for: (1) each proprietor, or (2) each limited partner who owns 20% or more interest and each general partner, or (3) each stockholder owning 20% or more of voting stock, or (4) any person or entity providing a guaranty on the loan.

Name	Business Phone
Residence Address	Residence Phone
City, State, & Zip Code	

Business Name of Applicant/Borrower

ASSETS (Omit Cents)		LIABILITIES (Omit Cents)	
Cash on hand & in Banks	$_____	Accounts Payable	$_____
Savings Accounts	$_____	Notes Payable to Banks and Others	$_____
IRA or Other Retirement Account	$_____	(Describe in Section 2)	
Accounts & Notes Receivable	$_____	Installment Account (Auto)	$_____
Life Insurance-Cash Surrender Value Only	$_____	Mo. Payments $_____	
(Complete Section 8)		Installment Account (Other)	$_____
Stocks and Bonds	$_____	Mo. Payments $_____	
(Describe in Section 3)		Loan on Life Insurance	$_____
Real Estate	$_____	Mortgages on Real Estate	$_____
(Describe in Section 4)		(Describe in Section 4)	
Automobile-Present Value	$_____	Unpaid Taxes	$_____
Other Personal Property	$_____	(Describe in Section 6)	
(Describe in Section 5)		Other Liabilities	$_____
Other Assets	$_____	(Describe in Section 7)	
(Describe in Section 5)		Total Liabilities	$_____
		Net Worth	$_____
Total	$_____	Total	$_____

Section 1. Source of Income		Contingent Liabilities	
Salary	$_____	As Endorser or Co-Maker	$_____
Net Investment Income	$_____	Legal Claims & Judgments	$_____
Real Estate Income	$_____	Provision for Federal Income Tax	$_____
Other Income (Describe below)*	$_____	Other Special Debt	$_____

Description of Other Income in Section 1.

*Alimony or child support payments need not be disclosed in "Other Income" unless it is desired to have such payments counted toward total income.

Section 2. Notes Payable to Banks and Others. (Use attachments if necessary. Each attachment must be identified as a part of this statement and signed.)

Name and Address of Noteholder(s)	Original Balance	Current Balance	Payment Amount	Frequency (monthly,etc.)	How Secured or Endorsed Type of Collateral

SBA Form 413 (3-00) **Previous Editions Obsolete**

This form was electronically produced by Elite Federal Forms, Inc.

(tumble)

Section 3. Stocks and Bonds. (Use attachments if necessary. Each attachment must be identified as a part of this statement and signed).

Number of Shares	Name of Securities	Cost	Market Value Quotation/Exchange	Date of Quotation/Exchange	Total Value

Section 4. Real Estate Owned.

(List each parcel separately. Use attachment if necessary. Each attachment must be identified as a part of this statement and signed.)

	Property A	Property B	Property C
Type of Property			
Address			
Date Purchased			
Original Cost			
Present Market Value			
Name & Address of Mortgage Holder			
Mortgage Account Number			
Mortgage Balance			
Amount of Payment per Month/Year			
Status of Mortgage			

Section 5. Other Personal Property and Other Assets.

(Describe, and if any is pledged as security, state name and address of lien holder, amount of lien, terms of payment and if delinquent, describe delinquency)

Section 6.   Unpaid Taxes.

(Describe in detail, as to type, to whom payable, when due, amount, and to what property, if any, a tax lien attaches.)

Section 7.   Other Liabilities.   (Describe in detail.)

Section 8.   Life Insurance Held.   (Give face amount and cash surrender value of policies - name of insurance company and beneficiaries)

I authorize SBA/Lender to make inquiries as necessary to verify the accuracy of the statements made and to determine my creditworthiness. I certify the above and the statements contained in the attachments are true and accurate as of the stated date(s). These statements are made for the purpose of either obtaining a loan or guaranteeing a loan. I understand FALSE statements may result in forfeiture of benefits and possible prosecution by the U.S. Attorney General (Reference 18 U.S.C. 1001).

Signature: Date: Social Security Number:

Signature: Date: Social Security Number:

PLEASE NOTE: The estimated average burden hours for the completion of this form is 1.5 hours per response. If you have questions or comments concerning this estimate or any other aspect of this information, please contact Chief, Administrative Branch, U.S. Small Business Administration, Washington, D.C. 20416, and Clearance Officer, Paper Reduction Project (3245-0188), Office of Management and Budget, Washington, D.C. 20503. **PLEASE DO NOT SEND FORMS TO OMB.**

START-UP COST WORKSHEET ●●●●●●

These are general expenses typically incurred during start-up and monthly operation. Please tailor this form to fit the requirements of your business.

START-UP DOLLARS NEEDED

Expense	Amount	Description
Advertising		Promotion for opening the business
Beginning Inventory		Amount of inventory needed to open
Building construction		Amount per contractor bid and other
Cash		Requirements for the cash register
Decorating		Estimate based on bid if applicable
Deposits		Check with utility companies
Fixtures and Equipment		Use actual bid on all fixtures and equipment
Installing fixtures and Equipment		Use actual bids and other
Insurance		Bid from insurance agent
Lease Payment		Amount to be paid before opening
Licenses and Permits		Check with city or state officials
Miscellaneous		All other
Professional Fees		Include coach, business consultant, accountant, attorney, engineer, etc.
Remodeling		Amount per contractor bid and other
Rent		Amount to be paid before opening
Services		Cleaning, accounting, etc.
Signs		Amount per contractor bid and other
Supplies		Office, cleaning, etc
Unanticipated Expenses		Include a reasonable amount for the unexpected
Other		
Other		
Other		
TOTAL START-UP DOLLARS	$	Total amount of costs before opening

REPEATING MONTHLY EXPENSES

In the repeating monthly expense include the first three months cash needs unless otherwise noted.

Expense	Amount	Description
Advertising		
Bank Service Charges		
Credit Card Fees		
Delivery Charges		
Donations/Charitable Giving		
Dues and Subscriptions		
Health Insurance		Not including the amount included above
Insurance		Not including the amount included above
Interest		
Inventory		*** See description below
Lease Payments		Not including the amount included above
Loan Payments		Principal and interest payments
Miscellaneous		
Office Expenses		
Payroll other than owner or manager		
Payroll Taxes		
Professional Fees		
Rent		Not including the amount included above
Repairs and Maintenance		
Salary of Owner and Manager		Include only if applicable for three months
Sales Tax		
Supplies		
Telephone		
Utilities		
Other		
Other		
Other		
Other		
Other		
Other		*** Include the amount that will be needed to expand your inventory. If inventory is to be replaced from cash sales do not include here. Assume the sale generated sufficient cash for the replacement.
TOTAL REPEATING EXPENSES	$	

TOTAL CASH NEEDED AT START-UP $

OPERATING EXPENSE FORECAST

	Actual	Estimate	Difference
Personnel Expenses			
Office			
Store			
Salespeople			
All Other			
Total			
Operating Expenses			
Advertising			
Bad Debts			
Cash Discounts			
Delivery			
Depreciation			
Donations			
Dues and Subscriptions			
Employee Benefits			
Insurance			
Interest			
Legal and Auditing			
Maintenance and Repairs			
Office Supplies			
Outboard Freight			
Postage			
Rent			
Sales Expenses			
Shipping/Storage			
Taxes			
Telephone			
Other:			
Total			

Source: Entrepreneur.com

EXPENSE REPORT

Employee's Name _____   From _____   To _____   Approved By _____

Expenditures* / Date	Monday	Tuesday	Wednesday	Thursday	Friday	Saturday	Sunday	Totals	Details/Description who and what discussed
Travel									
Hotel									
Phone									
Meals									
Breakfast									
Lunch									
Dinner									
Transportation									
Maintenance/Repair									
Wash									
Gas/Oil									
Airfare									
Taxi/Limo									
Car Rental									
Other Transportation									
Personal Car									
Tolls/Parking									
Business Entertainment									
Theatre									
Gifts									
Dinner									
Lunch									
Breakfast									
Miscellaneous									
Supplies									
Postage and Delivery									
Other, Miscellaneous									

Less Company Paid Transactions _____
Less Advance _____
Balance Returned or Due _____

Total Mileage This Report _____

*Retain receipts on all transactions with explanations

Source: Day Runner, Inc.

PETTY CASH VOUCHER

Date _____

Voucher Number _____

For	Account Debited	Account Number	Amount
		TOTAL	

Approved By _____

Received By _____

Date _____

Voucher Number _____

For	Account Debited	Account Number	Amount
		TOTAL	

Approved By _____

Received By _____

Source: Entrepreneur.com

PETTY CASH JOURNAL ●●●●●●

Reporting Period

From _____ To _____ Balance _____

Date	Voucher Number	Account Debited	Account Number	Payee	Approved By	Total	Balance

Audited By _____

Approved By _____

Total Voucher Amount		
Total Receipts		
Cash On Hand		
Overage/Shortage		
Petty Cash Reimbursement		
Balance Forward		

UNDERSTANDING THE BALANCE SHEET

The Balance Sheet shows the business' financial position as assets and liabilities at *a specified time*. A standard business plan includes a Projected Balance Sheet for a 12-month period for three years. However, for a start-up company the balance sheet will reflect your start-up cost while for an ongoing company it will show the ending balance from the previous year. The standard rule is that assets equal capital plus liabilities. If it does, it balances. *These estimates of assets, capital and liabilities come from your income statement and cash flow statement.*

Assets

1. *Cash Balance* – the accumulative balance in your business checking and savings account and petty cash.
2. *Accounts Receivable* – the money people owe you from sales already made. The balance increases with sales on credit and decreases when payments are received. For any given month, the ending balance is the sum of the previous ending balance, plus new sales on credit, minus payments received.
3. *Inventory* – previous balance minus direct cost of sales plus new inventory purchases.
4. *Other Current Assets* – Previous balance plus new assets purchased (use of cash) minus disposal (sale) of assets (source of cash)
5. *Capital Assets* – long-term assets (fixed assets), usually plant and equipment. Last month's balance plus new assets purchased minus disposal (sale) of assets.
6. *Accumulated Depreciation* – decreased the value of capital assets. Balance is equal to last month's balance plus new depreciation, from the income statement.

Liabilities

1. *Accounts Payable* – Last month's balance plus additions (a subset of costs and expenses) minus payment of payables. New payables are new inventory purchased on credit plus indirect costs of sales not paid when incurred, operating expense not paid when incurred and similar items.
2. *Current Notes* – Short-term notes equal to last month's balance plus new borrowing minus principal payments. Interest payments are not included because they go on the income statement and do not affect the balance. Principal payments and new borrowing should come from your cash flow statement.
3. *Other Current Liabilities* – accrued taxes, salary/payroll, and liabilities that have not been paid.
4. *Long-term Liabilities* – debt that increases when you borrow and decreases with principal payments. The balance is last month's balance plus new borrowing as a source of cash, minus principal payments as a use of cash.
5. *Paid-in Capital* – money invested. Last month's balance plus new investment from source of cash, minus dividends from uses of cash.
6. *Retained Earnings* – accumulated earnings reinvested in the company not taken out as dividends. Normally this changes once a year when annual statements are prepared.
7. *Earnings* – accumulated earnings since the end of the last year. The current month's balance is equal to last month's balance plus this month's earnings. At the end of the year, with an annual adjustment. Earnings still left in the business become retained earnings.

The Relationship Between the Balance Sheet and the Cash Flow Statement

- An increase in assets decreases your cash (Purchase). A decrease in assets increases your cash (Sale).
- An increase in liabilities increases cash (Owe). A decrease in liabilities decreases cash (Payment).

Remember, every dollar of receivables or inventory as assets is a dollar that you do not have in your cash balance. Likewise, every dollar in payables is a dollar that you have in cash.

Source: <u>Hurdle: the Book on Business Planning</u> by Tim Berry

THE BALANCE SHEET ●●●●●●

As of _____

ASSETS	
Cash Balance	
Accounts Receivable	
Inventory	
Total Assets	
CAPITAL AND LIABILITIES	
Liabilities	
Accounts Payable	
Short-term Debt	
Total Liabilities	
Capital	
Paid-in	
Earnings	
Total Capital and Liabilites	
NET WORTH	

THREE YEAR BALANCE SHEET

ASSETS	YEAR 1	YEAR 2	YEAR 3
Cash Balance			
Accounts Receivable			
Inventory			
Total Assets			
CAPITAL AND LIABILITIES			
Liabilities			
Accounts Payable			
Short-term Debt			
Total Liabilities			
Capital			
Paid-in			
Earnings			
Total Capital and Liabilites			
NET WORTH			

12 MONTH BALANCE SHEET ⚫⚫⚫⚫◯◯

ASSETS	Start	JAN	FEB	MAR	APR	MAY	JUN	JUL	AUG	SEP	OCT	NOV	DEC
Current Assets													
Cash Balance													
Accounts Receivable													
Inventory													
Other Current Assets													
Subtotal													
Capital Assets													
Accumulated Depreciation													
Subtotal													
Total Assets													
LIABILITIES													
Current Liabilities													
Accounts Payable													
Current Notes													
Other Current Liabilities													
Subtotal													
Long-term Liabilities													
Total Liabilities													
CAPITAL													
Paid-in Capital													
Retained Earnings													
Earnings													
Total Capital													
Total Capital and Liabilities													
NET WORTH													

65

SAMPLE BALANCE SHEET

	Dec 31, 99	Dec 31, 00	Dec 31, 01	Dec 31, 02	Dec 31, 03
ASSETS					
Current Assets					
Checking/Savings					
Company Checking Account	65,000	85,000	95,000	75,000	65,000
Company Savings Account	8,000	13,000	9,500	9,500	9,500
Petty Cash Account	-	500	500	500	500
Total Checking/Savings	73,000	98,500	105,000	85,000	75,000
Accounts Receivable	12,100	40,000	48,000	36,000	52,000
Total Accounts Receivable	12,100	40,000	48,000	36,000	52,000
Other Current Assets					
Inventory Asset	220,000	218,028	248,554	280,359	310,079
Prepaids	-	-	-	-	3,000
Security Deposit	1,000	1,000	3,000	3,000	3,000
Undeposited Funds	-	-	1,000	1,000	-
Total Other Current Assets	221,000	219,028	252,554	284,359	314,079
Total Current Assets	306,100	357,528	405,554	405,359	441,079
Fixed Assets					
Automobiles & Trucks	57,000	57,000	77,000	77,000	77,000
Computer & Office Equipment	-	2,500	5,000	5,000	7,500
Office Equipment (over $500)	5,500	5,500	7,000	7,000	9,000
Accumulated Depreciation	-	(923)	(154)	(154)	(154)
Total Fixed Assets	62,500	64,077	87,846	87,846	92,346
TOTAL ASSETS	368,600	421,605	493,400	493,205	533,425
LIABILITIES & EQUITY					
Liabilities					
Current Liabilities					
Accounts Payable	3,000	10,000	60,000	55,000	58,000
Total Accounts Payable	3,000	10,000	60,000	55,000	58,000
Credit Cards					
My Credit Card	-	600	250	250	300
Total Credit Cards	-	600	250	250	300
Other Liabilities					
Payroll Liabilities	-	1,500	2,500	3,000	3,500
Customer Deposits	33,000	30,000	25,000	35,000	45,000
Line of Credit	-	-	-	-	-
Total Other Current Liabilities	33,000	31,500	27,500	38,000	48,500
Total Current Liabilities	36,000	42,100	87,750	93,250	106,800
Long-Term Liabilities					
Long-Term Debt	105,000	105,000	105,000	115,000	115,000
Total Liabilities	141,000	147,100	192,750	208,250	221,800
Equity					
Capital	10,000	10,000	10,000	10,000	10,000
Retained Earnings	178,495	221,500	256,075	265,515	283,570
Net Income	39,105	43,005	34,575	9,440	18,055
Total Equity	227,600	274,505	300,650	284,955	311,625
TOTAL LIABILITIES & EQUITY	368,600	421,605	493,400	493,205	533,425

Source: "Beyond Survival: Strategic Financial Management" by Mathew J. Hultquist, CPA, PC, Greenville, SC

66

UNDERSTANDING THE 12 MONTH CASH FLOW STATEMENT

The cash flow statement is used to track the incoming and outgoing cash over a 12-month period. The cash flow statement is directly related to your balance sheet so be sure the two reflect consistency.

Source of Cash

1. *Cash Sales* – an estimate of the amount of cash you expect to receive from the sale of goods and/or services. It should be consistent with your sales forecast and income statement. Total cash sales reflects cash sales and sales on credit equal. Therefore cash refers to cash, check, and credit card, everything except actual credit sales where the customer is billed.
2. *From Receivables* – an estimate of the dollar amount received from customers as payments on accounts receivable.
3. *From Sale of Inventory* – reflects special sales of inventory outside of normal business sales. For example, a manufacturer may sell excess inventory of materials or components outside of its regular sales. This is not the same as the normal sale of inventory which goes on your income statement as sales.
4. *From Sale of Other Current Assets* and *From Sale of Capital Assets* – the sell of short-term and long-term assets is another source of cash.
5. *From New Short-term Debt* – an estimate of money borrowed through normal lending institutions, as standard loans with interest payments.
6. *From New Other Current Liabilities* – money accrued from taxes on sales, salaries, and wages. This is money owed that will have to be paid but is not formally borrowed. Normally there is no interest expense with this category.
7. *From New Long-term Debt* – money borrowed on longer terms.
8. *New Investments Received* – money coming in as an investment.

Use of Cash

1. *Pay Accounts Payable* – the accounts payable balance is money you owe that should be paid off every month.
2. *Payroll etc.* – wages, salaries, and other compensation-related payments you make every month to employees and the government. These obligations do not go in accounts payable and you pay them every month.
3. *Immediate Expenses* – these are expenses aside from wages that you pay as incurred so they never go into accounts payable.
4. *Immediate Cost of Sales* – instead of an expense this is the cost of sales, similar to the cost of goods sold.
5. *Interest Payments* – if interest is paid when incurred instead of waiting in payables to be paid later it should be accounted for here. This amount has to match the income statement.
6. *Principal Payments Short-term Debt* – principal payment on short-term debt.
7. *Principal Payments Long-term Debt* – principal payments on long-term debt.
8. *Inventory Paid in Cash* – You will have to know how much new inventory you will buy, so the portion of it paid in the same month is part of calculating new payables.
9. *New Capital Assets* – asset purchases reduce cash and change the balance sheet amount for related assets.

continued

Source: <u>Hurdle: the Book on Business Planning</u> by Tim Berry

Calculating the Cash Balance

To calculate, add the new sources of cash and subtract the uses of cash and you will have a monthly estimate for Cash Balance. You may need to tailor your cash flow statement by adding categories to reflect the specific inflows and outflows that reduce cash. Other items that may be seen are the Purchase of Short-term Assets, Owner's Draw (money you take out for whatever reason) or Dividends, Interest Income, and Miscellaneous Income.

Source: Hurdle: the Book on Business Planning by Tim Berry

12 MONTH CASH FLOW STATEMENT

SOURCE OF CASH	JAN	FEB	MAR	APR	MAY	JUN	JUL	AUG	SEP	OCT	NOV	DEC
Cash Sales												
From Receivables												
From Sale of Inventory												
From Sale of Other Current Assets												
From Sale of Capital Assets												
From New Short-term Debt												
From New Other Current Liabilities												
From New Long-term Debt												
New Investments Received												
Total Inflow												
USE OF CASH												
Pay Accounts Payable												
Payroll etc.												
Immediate Expenses												
Immediate Cost of Sales												
Interest Payments												
Principal Payments Short-term Debt												
Principal Payments Long-term Debt												
Inventory Paid in Cash												
New Capital Assets												
Total Outflow												
Cash Flow												
Cash Balance												

UNDERSTANDING THE PROFIT LOSS STATEMENT ⬤⬤⬤⬤●●

The Profit Loss Statement *also known as the Income Statement* shows you "the bottom line"; profits. Profits are what is left after you subtract the cost of sales, expenses, and taxes from sales. Expenses include but are not limited to personnel, rent, utilities, equipment, advertising, commissions, and public relations.

You may also see this statement referred to as a "pro forma income statement" or "pro forma profit loss statement". The pro forma income statement is the same as a standard income statement except that the standard statement shows actual results from the past, while the pro forma statement projects the future.

There is typically a line entry on the income statement called "gross margin". The income statement following does not include gross margin however, gross margin is the difference between total sales revenue and total cost of goods sold (also called total cost of sales). If you would like to include gross margin enter the following line items after Income before Expenses: Total Cost of Sales, Gross Margin and Gross Margin %. This can also be expressed in dollar or percentage terms and on a per unit basis, as the difference between unit selling price and unit cost of goods sold. Acceptable levels depend on the nature of the business. For example, according to the 1997 Financial Statement Studies of Robert Morris Associates, and average shoe store has a gross margin of 42 percent. A grocery store about 20 percent and a hat manufacturer about 30 percent. There are providers who can deliver standard gross margins for different types of industries based on SIC (Standard Industry Classification) codes that categorize industries.

If you prefer to use an income statement that depicts gross margin, it can be calculated in dollars by:
Total Sales – Cost of Sales = Gross Margin
$85,000 - $24,000 = $61,000

It can be expressed as a percentage by:
100 – (Cost of Sales/Total Sales)(100) = Gross Margin Percentage
100 – ($24,000/$85,000)(100)
100 – (0.2823529)(100)
100 – 28.23529
= 71.76%

Planned vs. Actual Profit Loss

Your profit loss statement is a means to budget and forecast your expenses. Therefore it is important to track sales, expenses, and taxes and review and enter actual numbers in the table to maintain an accurate picture of spending and profit. Even if the business is doing well and you see profits and the cash flow is satisfactory it is still very important to planning to track actual outcomes at the end of the month. Tracking outcomes in a computer based spreadsheet will make this process easier and less time consuming. When you review the variance between actual and planned numbers, ask yourself what that difference means to the business. A positive balance, in theory, is good news because it means you spent less than budgeted. Conversely, a negative variance means you spent more than the budget. However positive variances aren't always good news. If you planned to spend $5,000 in advertising and the money was not spent that means you did no advertising. Suppose sales are also low for the following month, could this be as a result of no advertising? Every variance should provoke questions. Why did one project cost more or less? Were objectives met? Is a positive variance (under budget) a cost saving or a failure to implement? Is a negative variance (over budget) a change in plans, a management failure, or an unrealistic budget? As you can see, a variance table can provide you with significant information so these important questions don't go unasked. In evaluating variance, whether the numbers are positive or negative, the real test is whether or not the result was good for the business.

Source: <u>Hurdle: the Book on Business Planning</u> by Tim Berry

PROFIT LOSS STATEMENT

	JAN	FEB	MAR	APR	MAY	JUN	JUL	AUG	SEP	OCT	NOV	DEC
INCOME												
Gross Sales												
Less returns												
Less Discounts												
Less Debts												
Interest, Rent, Royalties												
Total Income												
EXPENSES												
Cost of Goods Sold												
Direct Payroll												
Indirect Payroll												
Taxes other than income tax												
Sales Expenses												
Postage and Shipping												
Advertising and Promotion												
Office Expenses												
Travel and Entertainment												
Phone												
Other Utilities												
Automobile												
Insurance												
Professional Fees												
Rent												
Interest on Loans												
Other, Miscellaneous												
Total Expenses												
Net Income												
Less Income Taxes												
NET INCOME AFTER TAXES												

71

SAMPLE PROFIT LOSS STATEMENT

	Jan - Dec 99	Jan - Dec 00	Jan - Dec 01	Jan - Dec 02	Jan - Dec 03	TOTAL
Ordinary Income/Expense						
Income						
Pool Cover & Equipment Sales	377,000	395,000	405,000	425,000	435,000	2,037,000
Revenue - Installation Service	16,000	18,000	20,000	25,000	27,500	106,500
Revenue - Repair Service	300	500	750	1,500	1,600	4,650
Total Income	393,300	413,500	425,750	451,500	464,100	2,148,150
Cost of Goods Sold						
Inventory Overages/Shortages	420	20	150	550	400	1,540
Materials	188,000	195,000	204,000	236,000	238,000	1,061,000
Direct Labor	59,000	65,000	68,000	79,000	80,000	351,000
Freight	250	350	500	1,000	1,000	3,100
Fall Out/Spoilage	500	100	150	75	100	925
Total COGS	248,170	260,470	272,800	316,625	319,500	1,417,565
Gross Profit	145,130	153,030	152,950	134,875	144,600	730,585
Expense						
Advertising Expense	1,825	2,500	2,750	3,100	3,300	13,475
Business License & Fees	710	50	75	50	100	985
Car/Truck Expense	13,810	14,500	15,750	16,500	16,600	77,160
Conferences and Seminars	575	0	650	0	0	1,225
Contributions	1,000	0	500	100	0	1,600
Depreciation Expense	920	920	920	920	920	4,600
Dues and Subscriptions	1,220	1,000	1,100	800	1,250	5,370
Insurance	28,500	31,000	33,500	34,500	34,500	162,000
Maintenance/Janitorial	1,200	1,200	1,350	1,360	1,400	6,510
Tools & Equipment Expense	620	750	880	900	1,400	4,550
Meals	1,375	900	650	780	400	4,105
Office Equipment	1,075	650	850	400	750	3,725
Postage and Delivery	1,100	1,600	1,750	1,800	1,850	8,100
Professional Fees	4,100	4,350	4,550	4,500	4,100	21,600
Promotional Expense	350	0	0	100	0	450
Rent	7,005	7,005	7,100	7,100	7,250	35,460
Repairs	390	150	200	225	650	1,615
Supplies	2,800	3,000	2,900	2,200	2,350	13,250
Telephone	3,000	3,350	3,550	3,600	3,425	16,925
Travel & Entertainment	950	500	600	1,000	300	3,350
Wages	33,000	36,000	38,000	45,000	46,000	198,000
Utilities	500	600	750	500	0	2,350
Total Expense	106,025	110,025	118,375	125,435	126,545	586,405
Net Ordinary Income	39,105	43,005	34,575	9,440	18,055	144,180
Net Income	39,105	43,005	34,575	9,440	18,055	144,180

Source: "Beyond Survival: Strategic Financial Management" by Mathew J. Hultquist, CPA, PC, c

GENERAL JOURNAL

MONTH _____

GENERAL LEDGER NUMBER _____

Date	Amount Debited	Account Number	Amount	Account Credited	Account Number	Amount

General Journal: used to record monthly transactions for a variety of accounts.

Source: Entrepreneur.com

GENERAL LEDGER ●●●●●●

MONTH _____   ACCOUNT NAME _____

GENERAL LEDGER NUMBER _____   ACCOUNT NUMBER _____

Date	Item	Transaction		Balance	
		Debit	Credit	Debit	Credit

General Ledger: used to provide a monthly list of activity and balances for a specific account.

RETENTION RECORD

The following chart indicates how long you should keep certain business and financial records.

Record Type	How Long?
Correspondence (routine) with customers or vendors	1 year
Employment Applications	1 year
Purchase order (except purchasing department copy)	1 year
Requisitions	1 year
Stenographers notebooks	1 year
Stockroom withdrawal forms	1 year
Bank reconciliations	2 years
Correspondence (general)	2 years
Duplicate deposit slips	2 years
Bank statements	3 years
Employee personnel records (after termination)	3 years
Insurance policies (expired)	3 years
Internal audit reports (in some situations, longer)	3 years
Internal reports (miscellaneous)	3 years
Monthly financial statements	3 years
Petty cash vouchers	3 years
Physical inventory tags	3 years
Savings bond registration records of employees	3 years
Sub ledgers	3 years
Sales records such as invoices, monthly statements, remittance advisories, shipping papers, bills of lading and customers' purchase orders	6 years
Travel and entertainment records, including account books, diaries and expense statements and receipts	6 years
Inventory records	7 years
Accident report and claims (settled cases)	7 years
Accounts payable ledgers and schedules	7 years
Accounts receivable ledgers and schedules	7 years
Inventory records	7 years
Notes receivable ledgers and schedules	7 years
Patient charts	7 years
Payroll records and summaries including payments for pensioners and dividends	7 years

RETENTION RECORD ●●●●●●

The following chart indicates how long you should keep certain business and financial records.

Record Type	How Long?
Stock and bond certificates canceled	7 years
Property appraisals by outside appraisers	7 years
Capital stock and bond records; ledgers transfer registers, stub showing issues, record of interest coupons, options, etc.	Permanently
Cash books	Permanently
Chart of accounts	Permanently
Contracts, notes, and leases (in effect)	Permanently
Correspondence (legal, i.e. protests, court briefs, appeal, and important matters only)	Permanently
Audit report of accountant	Permanently
Checks (canceled for important payments, i.e. taxes, purchase of property, special contracts, etc. Checks should be filed with the papers pertaining to the underlying transaction	Permanently
Tax returns and work sheets, revenue agent's reports and other documents relating to determination of income tax liability	Permanently
Financial Statements (end-of-year, other months optional)	Permanently
General and private ledgers (and end-of-year trail balances)	Permanently
Insurance records, current accident reports, claims, policies, etc.	Permanently
Deeds, mortgages, and bills of sales	Permanently
Documents substantiating fixed-asset additions and salvage values assigned to assets	Permanently
Property appraisals by outside appraisers	Permanently
Property records – including costs, depreciation reserves, end of year trial balances, depreciation, schedules, blue prints and plans	Permanently
Journals	Permanently
Minute book for directors and stockholders, including by-laws and charter	Permanently
Depreciation schedules	Permanently
Corporate documents, including certificates of incorporation, corporate charter, constitution and bylaws, deeds and easements, stock, stock transfer records, minutes of board of director meetings, retirement and pension records, labor contracts and license, patent, trademark and registration applications	Permanently

Source: Entrepreneur.com, Dixon Hughes, Greenville, SC

SBA/BANK FINANCING CHECKLIST ●●●●●●

This is a checklist provided by the Small Business Administration (SBA) to inform you of the required documentation necessary to apply for financing from the SBA or a bank. Some banks may vary on the documentation required or provide their own forms. To obtain the SBA forms mentioned below go to www.sba.gov/library/forms.html. If you do not plan to seek financing from the SBA or a bank at this time, this checklist is a good reference for the type of records and documentation your company should keep in order to be organizationally sound and considered for financing.

1. Application for Loan: SBA form 4, 4I

2. Statement of Personal History: SBA form 912

3. Personal Financial Statement: SBA form 413

4. Detailed, signed Balance Sheet and Profit & Loss Statements current (within 90 days of application) and last three (3) fiscal years Supplementary Schedules required on Current Financial Statements.

5. Detailed one (1) year projection of Income & Finances (please attach written explanation as to how you expect to achieve same).

6. A list of names and addresses of any subsidiaries and affiliates, including concerns in which the applicant holds a controlling (but not necessarily a majority) interest and other concerns that may be affiliated by stock ownership, franchise, proposed merger or otherwise with the applicant.

7. Certificate of Doing Business (If a corporation, stamp corporate seal on SBA form 4 section 12).

8. By Law, the Agency may not guarantee a loan if a business can obtain funds on reasonable terms from a bank or other private source. A borrower therefore must first seek private financing.

    A company must be independently owned and operated, not dominant in its field and must meet certain standards of size in terms of employees or annual receipts. Loans cannot b made to speculative businesses, newspapers, or businesses engaged in gambling.

    Applicants for loans must also agree to comply with SBA regulation that there will be no discrimination in employment or services to the public, based on race, color, religion, national origin, sex or marital status.

9. Signed Business Federal Income Tax Returns for previous three (3) year.

10. Signed Personal Federal Income Tax Returns of principals for previous three (3) years.

11. Personal Resume including business experience of each principal.

12. Brief history of the business and its problems:

13. Include an explanation of why the SBA loan is needed and how it will help the business.

14. Copy of Business Lease (or note from landlord giving terms of proposed lease.

15. For purchase of an existing business:
    a. Current Balance Sheet and Profit & Loss Statement of business to be purchased.
    b. Previous two (2) years Federal Income Tax Returns of the business.
    c. Propose Bill of Sale Including: Terms of Sale.
    d. Asking Price with schedule of:
        1. Inventory
        2. Machinery & Equipment
        3. Furniture & Fixtures

Source: U.S. Small Business Administration. www.sba.gov

TAX INCENTIVES ●●●●●●●

❶ *What is -- and isn't -- a tax-deductible business expense?*

- ✓ Tax-deductible business expenses are generally defined as any "ordinary, necessary and reasonable" expense that helps you earn business income.
- ✓ When buying goods, the items must be used in a "trade or business," which means it is used with the expectation of generating income.
- ✓ Non-deductible expenses that your business may incur are:
  - o A bribe paid to a public official
  - o Traffic tickets
  - o Home telephone line
  - o Clothing you wear on the job, unless it is a required uniform

❷ *If I use my car for business, how much of that expense can I write off?*

You must keep track of how much you use your car for business in order to figure out your deduction and maintain written records. There are two methods:

- ✓ Mileage Method - keep a log showing the miles for each business use, always noting the purpose of the trip. Deduct a certain dollar amount based on this IRS rate:
  - o 37.5 cents in 2004
- ✓ Actual Expense Method - deduct the actual costs you incur each year to operate your car plus depreciation for gas and repairs according to a tax code schedule. Deductible expenses are: multiplied by the percentage of business use you can deduct the total you pay for:
  - o Gas and oil
  - o Repairs and maintenance
  - o Depreciation
  - o License fees
  - o Insurance
  - o Tolls
  - o Car washing
- ✓ Under the actual expense method, if the car is also used for personal use, you must multiply your actual expenses by the percentage of business use.

Figure it both ways and use the method that benefits you more.

❸ *Can I claim a deduction for business-related entertainment?*

You may deduct only 50% of expenses for entertaining clients or customers for business purposes. Qualified business entertainment includes:

- ✓ Taking a client to a sporting event
- ✓ A concert
- ✓ Dinner at a restaurant
- ✓ Inviting a few of your customers over for a weekend barbecue at your home. Parties, picnics and other social events you hold for your employees and their families are an exception to the 50% rule -- such events are 100% deductible.

Remember, if you are audited, you must be able to show proof that the entertainment expense was either directly related to, or associated with business. So, keep a guest list and note the business (or potential) relationship of each person entertained.

❹ *When can you deduct 100% of business supplies and equipment in the year they are purchased, and when do you have to deduct the purchase price over several years?*

Current expenses or everyday costs of keeping your business going are 100% deductible in the year you incur them:

- ✓ Office supplies
- ✓ Rent and electricity

Capital expenses, expenditures for things that will help to generate revenue in future years must be written off over their useful life – three, five, or seven years. The following are examples:

- ✓ Desk
- ✓ Copier
- ✓ Car

There is one important exception to this rule, called the Section 179 deduction, which may let you deduct even capital expenses in the year you incur them. (See Current vs. Capitalized Expenses at www.nolo.com for more information.)

❺ *If I buy a new computer system, office furniture or equipment this year, do I have to spread the deduction over a period of five years?*

While the cost of "capital equipment" -- equipment that has a useful life of more than one year, such as a computer system -- must normally be deducted over a number of years, there is one major exception. Internal Revenue Code Section 179 allows you to deduct a certain amount of capital assets per year against your business income. In 2003, the limit increased from $24,000 to $100,000; the limit is $102,000 for 2004 and 2005.   However, this limit is scheduled to go back down to $25,000 in 2006 although Congress could decide to make the higher limit permanent.

Note: You can still qualify for this deduction even if you buy a computer system on credit with no money down. Section 179 does not apply to land, buildings, inventory, intangible assets, air conditioning, heating units or vehicles, but remember, special rules limit the portion of the cost of a car that you can depreciate each year. For more information, see Deduct It!: Lower Your Small Business Taxes, by Stephen Fishman at www.nolo.com.

❻ *I am planning a trip to a trade show. Can I take my family along for a vacation and still be able to deduct the expenses?*

If you take others with you on a business trip, you can deduct business expenses for the trip no greater than if you were traveling alone. For example, If your family rides in the back seat of the car and stays in one standard motel room, then you can fully deduct your automobile and hotel expenses. But you can't claim a deduction for your family's meals or a break to an amusement park.

You can fully deduct:

- ✓ The cost of your airline ticket even if it features a two-for-one or "companion" discount.
- ✓ If you extend your stay and partake in some of the fun after the business is over, the expenses attributed to the non-business days <u>aren't deductible</u>, unless you extended your stay to get discounted airfare (the "Saturday overnight" requirement). In this case, your hotel room and meals would be fully deductible.

❼ *I work in my home part-time. Can I take the home-office tax deduction?*

If you run a business out of your home, you can usually claim a deduction of rental or mortgages cost and also for the portion of the home used for business. Additionally, you can deduct related costs utilities, insurance, and remodeling.

You will not qualify if you work part time at home because your primary office is elsewhere, or if you use your den partly for work and partly for personal use.

There is a disadvantage of taking these deductions. You may end up paying extra taxes when you sell your house -- if you don't live in your house in two of the last five years before you sell the house. For more information, see The Home-Office Tax Deduction at www.nolo.com or check with a tax professional.

❽ *Does incorporating a small business start-up offer tax breaks?*

Companies with cash flow and substantial profits benefit from incorporation. Few start-ups have the cash flow needed to take advantage of corporate tax breaks. Therefore, profitable, established corporations, not to start-ups in their first few years receive corporate tax benefits. For example, corporations can offer more tax-flexible pension plans than sole proprietors or partnerships.

Similarly, the ability to split income between a corporation and its owners -- thereby keeping some income in lower corporate tax brackets -- is effective only if the business is solidly profitable. (See Cut Taxes With Corporate Income Splitting for more information at www.nolo.com)

In addition, incorporating adds state fees, as well as legal and accounting charges. So unless you are sure that will receive an immediate profit, you may want to wait to incorporate your business.

❾ *Is it safe and sensible for me to keep my own books and file my own tax returns?*

Forms have been included in this guide for manual bookkeeping and reference. However, to keep your own books, consider using a check-register type computer program such as Quicken Home & Business or Quickbooks (by Intuit) to track your expenses. If you are doing your own tax return, TurboTax is compatible with these programs.

Always check with a small business accountant and/or bookkeeper to make sure you're on the right track and meeting tax filing requirements.

TAX INCENTIVES ●●●●●●

I need to hire people quickly for a big job coming up. Should I hire independent contractors or new employees?

If you will be telling your workers where, when, and how to do their jobs, you should treat them as employees, because that is how the IRS will classify them. An independent contractors or freelancers own their own business and offer their services to several clients.

Classifying your workers as contractors would save you money in the short run because you wouldn't have to pay the employer's share of payroll taxes or have an accountant keep records and file payroll tax forms. But if the IRS later audits you and reclassifies your "independent contractors" as employees and assess hefty back taxes, penalties, and interest against you. If in doubt, treat workers as employees.

Keep all receipts and canceled checks for business expenses, and keep them organized, in a safe place, and into individual folders or envelopes. Separate the documents by category, such as:

- Auto Expenses
- Advertising
- Rent
- Professional Fees
- Travel
- Entertainment
- Utilities

Tax Deductible Expenses Include (please consult an accountant, there are specifics you must follow depending on the type of business and the type of expense)

Auto Expenses	Professional Development	Advertising, Promotion and Publicity
Bad Debts	Bank Service Charges	Business Association Dues
Business Entertaining	Business Gifts	Business-Related Magazines and Books
Casual Labor and Tips	Casualty and Theft Losses	Charitable Contributions
Coffee and Beverage Service	Commissions	Consultant Fees
Credit Bureau Fees	Education Expenses	Interest
Legal and Professional Fees	Moving Expenses	New Equipment
Office Supplies	Online Computer Services	Parking and Meters
Petty Cash Funds	Postage	Utilities
Seminars and Trade Shows	Software	Taxi and Bus Fare
Taxes	Telephone Calls	Travel

Source: www.nolo.com

Form **SS-4**
(Rev. December 2001)
Department of the Treasury
Internal Revenue Service

Application for Employer Identification Number

(For use by employers, corporations, partnerships, trusts, estates, churches, government agencies, Indian tribal entities, certain individuals, and others.)

▶ See separate instructions for each line.   ▶ Keep a copy for your records.

EIN

OMB No. 1545-0003

Type or print clearly.

1 Legal name of entity (or individual) for whom the EIN is being requested

2 Trade name of business (if different from name on line 1)

3 Executor, trustee, "care of" name

4a Mailing address (room, apt., suite no. and street, or P.O. box)

5a Street address (if different) (Do not enter a P.O. box.)

4b City, state, and ZIP code

5b City, state, and ZIP code

6 County and state where principal business is located

7a Name of principal officer, general partner, grantor, owner, or trustor

7b SSN, ITIN, or EIN

8a Type of entity (check only one box)
- ☐ Sole proprietor (SSN) _____
- ☐ Partnership
- ☐ Corporation (enter form number to be filed) ▶ _____
- ☐ Personal service corp.
- ☐ Church or church-controlled organization
- ☐ Other nonprofit organization (specify) ▶ _____
- ☐ Other (specify) ▶

- ☐ Estate (SSN of decedent) _____
- ☐ Plan administrator (SSN) _____
- ☐ Trust (SSN of grantor) _____
- ☐ National Guard   ☐ State/local government
- ☐ Farmers' cooperative   ☐ Federal government/military
- ☐ REMIC   ☐ Indian tribal governments/enterprises
- Group Exemption Number (GEN) ▶ _____

8b If a corporation, name the state or foreign country (if applicable) where incorporated

State

Foreign country

9 Reason for applying (check only one box)
- ☐ Started new business (specify type) ▶ _____
- ☐ Hired employees (Check the box and see line 12.)
- ☐ Compliance with IRS withholding regulations
- ☐ Other (specify) ▶

- ☐ Banking purpose (specify purpose) ▶ _____
- ☐ Changed type of organization (specify new type) ▶ _____
- ☐ Purchased going business
- ☐ Created a trust (specify type) ▶ _____
- ☐ Created a pension plan (specify type) ▶ _____

10 Date business started or acquired (month, day, year)

11 Closing month of accounting year

12 First date wages or annuities were paid or will be paid (month, day, year). **Note:** *If applicant is a withholding agent, enter date income will first be paid to nonresident alien. (month, day, year)* . . . . . ▶

13 Highest number of employees expected in the next 12 months. **Note:** *If the applicant does not expect to have any employees during the period, enter "-0-."* . . . . ▶

Agricultural	Household	Other

14 Check **one** box that best describes the principal activity of your business.
- ☐ Construction   ☐ Rental & leasing   ☐ Transportation & warehousing
- ☐ Real estate   ☐ Manufacturing   ☐ Finance & insurance
- ☐ Health care & social assistance   ☐ Wholesale–agent/broker
- ☐ Accommodation & food service   ☐ Wholesale–other   ☐ Retail
- ☐ Other (specify)

15 Indicate principal line of merchandise sold; specific construction work done; products produced; or services provided.

16a Has the applicant ever applied for an employer identification number for this or any other business? . . . . ☐ **Yes**   ☐ **No**
Note: *If "Yes," please complete lines 16b and 16c.*

16b If you checked "Yes" on line 16a, give applicant's legal name and trade name shown on prior application if different from line 1 or 2 above.
Legal name ▶   Trade name ▶

16c Approximate date when, and city and state where, the application was filed. Enter previous employer identification number if known.
Approximate date when filed (mo., day, year)   City and state where filed   Previous EIN

Third Party Designee

Complete this section **only** if you want to authorize the named individual to receive the entity's EIN and answer questions about the completion of this form.

Designee's name

Designee's telephone number (include area code)
( )

Address and ZIP code

Designee's fax number (include area code)
( )

Under penalties of perjury, I declare that I have examined this application, and to the best of my knowledge and belief, it is true, correct, and complete.

Applicant's telephone number (include area code)
( )

Name and title (type or print clearly) ▶

Applicant's fax number (include area code)
( )

Signature ▶   Date ▶

For Privacy Act and Paperwork Reduction Act Notice, see separate instructions.   Cat. No. 16055N   Form **SS-4** (Rev. 12-2001)

Do I Need an EIN?

File Form SS-4 if the applicant entity does not already have an EIN but is required to show an EIN on any return, statement, or other document.[1] **See also the separate instructions for each line on Form SS-4.**

IF the applicant...	AND...	THEN...
Started a new business	Does not currently have (nor expect to have) employees	Complete lines 1, 2, 4a–6, 8a, and 9–16c.
Hired (or will hire) employees, including household employees	Does not already have an EIN	Complete lines 1, 2, 4a–6, 7a–b (if applicable), 8a, 8b (if applicable), and 9–16c.
Opened a bank account	Needs an EIN for banking purposes only	Complete lines 1–5b, 7a–b (if applicable), 8a, 9, and 16a–c.
Changed type of organization	Either the legal character of the organization or its ownership changed (e.g., you incorporate a sole proprietorship or form a partnership)[2]	Complete lines 1–16c (as applicable).
Purchased a going business[3]	Does not already have an EIN	Complete lines 1–16c (as applicable).
Created a trust	The trust is other than a grantor trust or an IRA trust[4]	Complete lines 1–16c (as applicable).
Created a pension plan as a plan administrator[5]	Needs an EIN for reporting purposes	Complete lines 1, 2, 4a–6, 8a, 9, and 16a–c.
Is a foreign person needing an EIN to comply with IRS withholding regulations	Needs an EIN to complete a Form W-8 (other than Form W-8ECI), avoid withholding on portfolio assets, or claim tax treaty benefits[6]	Complete lines 1–5b, 7a–b (SSN or ITIN optional), 8a–9, and 16a–c.
Is administering an estate	Needs an EIN to report estate income on Form 1041	Complete lines 1, 3, 4a–b, 8a, 9, and 16a–c.
Is a withholding agent for taxes on non-wage income paid to an alien (i.e., individual, corporation, or partnership, etc.)	Is an agent, broker, fiduciary, manager, tenant, or spouse who is required to file **Form 1042,** Annual Withholding Tax Return for U.S. Source Income of Foreign Persons	Complete lines 1, 2, 3 (if applicable), 4a–5b, 7a–b (if applicable), 8a, 9, and 16a–c.
Is a state or local agency	Serves as a tax reporting agent for public assistance recipients under Rev. Proc. 80-4, 1980-1 C.B. 581[7]	Complete lines 1, 2, 4a–5b, 8a, 9, and 16a–c.
Is a single-member LLC	Needs an EIN to file **Form 8832,** Classification Election, for filing employment tax returns, **or** for state reporting purposes[8]	Complete lines 1–16c (as applicable).
Is an S corporation	Needs an EIN to file **Form 2553,** Election by a Small Business Corporation[9]	Complete lines 1–16c (as applicable).

[1] For example, a sole proprietorship or self-employed farmer who establishes a qualified retirement plan, or is required to file excise, employment, alcohol, tobacco, or firearms returns, must have an EIN. **A partnership, corporation, REMIC (real estate mortgage investment conduit), nonprofit organization (church, club, etc.), or farmers' cooperative must use an EIN for any tax-related purpose even if the entity does not have employees.**

[2] However, **do not** apply for a new EIN if the existing entity only **(a)** changed its business name, **(b)** elected on Form 8832 to change the way it is taxed (or is covered by the default rules), or **(c)** terminated its partnership status because at least 50% of the total interests in partnership capital and profits were sold or exchanged within a 12-month period. (The EIN of the terminated partnership should continue to be used. See Regulations section 301.6109-1(d)(2)(iii).)

[3] Do not use the EIN of the prior business unless you became the "owner" of a corporation by acquiring its stock.

[4] However, IRA trusts that are required to file **Form 990-T,** Exempt Organization Business Income Tax Return, must have an EIN.

[5] A plan administrator is the person or group of persons specified as the administrator by the instrument under which the plan is operated.

[6] Entities applying to be a Qualified Intermediary (QI) need a QI-EIN even if they already have an EIN. **See Rev. Proc. 2000-12.**

[7] See also *Household employer* on page 4. (**Note:** State or local agencies may need an EIN for other reasons, e.g., hired employees.)

[8] Most LLCs **do not** need to file Form 8832. See **Limited liability company (LLC)** on page 4 for details on completing Form SS-4 for an LLC.

[9] An existing corporation that is electing or revoking S corporation status should use its previously-assigned EIN.

Instructions for Form SS-4
(Rev. September 2003)

Department of the Treasury
Internal Revenue Service

For use with Form SS-4 (Rev. December 2001)
Application for Employer Identification Number.
Section references are to the Internal Revenue Code unless otherwise noted.

General Instructions

Use these instructions to complete **Form SS-4,** Application for Employer Identification Number. Also see **Do I Need an EIN?** on page 2 of Form SS-4.

Purpose of Form

Use Form SS-4 to apply for an employer identification number (EIN). An EIN is a nine-digit number (for example, 12-3456789) assigned to sole proprietors, corporations, partnerships, estates, trusts, and other entities for tax filing and reporting purposes. The information you provide on this form will establish your business tax account.

> **⚠ CAUTION**
> *An EIN is for use in connection with your business activities only. Do **not** use your EIN in place of your social security number (SSN).*

Items To Note

Apply online. You can now apply for and receive an EIN online using the internet. See **How To Apply** below.

File only one Form SS-4. Generally, a sole proprietor should file only one Form SS-4 and needs only one EIN, regardless of the number of businesses operated as a sole proprietorship or trade names under which a business operates. However, if the proprietorship incorporates or enters into a partnership, a new EIN is required. Also, each corporation in an affiliated group must have its own EIN.

EIN applied for, but not received. If you do not have an EIN by the time a return is due, write "Applied For" and the date you applied in the space shown for the number. **Do not** show your SSN as an EIN on returns.

If you do not have an EIN by the time a tax deposit is due, send your payment to the Internal Revenue Service Center for your filing area as shown in the instructions for the form that you are filing. Make your check or money order payable to the "United States Treasury" and show your name (as shown on Form SS-4), address, type of tax, period covered, and date you applied for an EIN.

How To Apply

You can apply for an EIN online, by telephone, by fax, or by mail depending on how soon you need to use the EIN. Use only one method for each entity so you do not receive more than one EIN for an entity.

Online. You can receive your EIN by internet and use it immediately to file a return or make a payment. Go to the IRS website at **www.irs.gov/businesses** and click on **Employer ID Numbers** under **topics.**

Telephone. You can receive your EIN by telephone and use it immediately to file a return or make a payment. Call the IRS at **1-800-829-4933.** (International applicants must call 215-516-6999.) The hours of operation are 7:00 a.m. to 10:00 p.m. The person making the call must be authorized to sign the form or be an authorized designee. See **Signature** and **Third Party Designee** on page 6. Also see the **TIP** below.

If you are applying by telephone, it will be helpful to complete Form SS-4 before contacting the IRS. An IRS representative will use the information from the Form SS-4 to establish your account and assign you an EIN. Write the number you are given on the upper right corner of the form and sign and date it. Keep this copy for your records.

If requested by an IRS representative, mail or fax (facsimile) the signed Form SS-4 (including any Third Party Designee authorization) within 24 hours to the IRS address provided by the IRS representative.

> **TIP**
> *Taxpayer representatives can apply for an EIN on behalf of their client and request that the EIN be faxed to their **client** on the same day. **Note:** By using this procedure, you are authorizing the IRS to fax the EIN without a cover sheet.*

Fax. Under the Fax-TIN program, you can receive your EIN by fax within 4 business days. Complete and fax Form SS-4 to the IRS using the Fax-TIN number listed on page 2 for your state. A long-distance charge to callers outside of the local calling area will apply. Fax-TIN numbers can only be used to apply for an EIN. **The numbers may change without notice.** Fax-TIN is available 24 hours a day, 7 days a week.

Be sure to provide your fax number so the IRS can fax the EIN back to you. **Note:** By using this procedure, you are authorizing the IRS to fax the EIN without a cover sheet.

Mail. Complete Form SS-4 at least 4 to 5 weeks before you will need an EIN. Sign and date the application and mail it to the service center address for your state. You will receive your EIN in the mail in approximately 4 weeks. See also **Third Party Designee** on page 6.

Call 1-800-829-4933 to verify a number or to ask about the status of an application by mail.

If your principal business, office or agency, or legal residence in the case of an individual, is located in:	Call the Fax-TIN number shown or file with the "Internal Revenue Service Center" at:
Connecticut, Delaware, District of Columbia, Florida, Georgia, Maine, Maryland, Massachusetts, New Hampshire, New Jersey, New York, North Carolina, Ohio, Pennsylvania, Rhode Island, South Carolina, Vermont, Virginia, West Virginia	Attn: EIN Operation P. O. Box 9003 Holtsville, NY 11742-9003 Fax-TIN 631-447-8960
Illinois, Indiana, Kentucky, Michigan	Attn: EIN Operation Cincinnati, OH 45999 Fax-TIN 859-669-5760
Alabama, Alaska, Arizona, Arkansas, California, Colorado, Hawaii, Idaho, Iowa, Kansas, Louisiana, Minnesota, Mississippi, Missouri, Montana, Nebraska, Nevada, New Mexico, North Dakota, Oklahoma, Oregon, Puerto Rico, South Dakota, Tennessee, Texas, Utah, Washington, Wisconsin, Wyoming	Attn: EIN Operation Philadelphia, PA 19255 Fax-TIN 215-516-3990
If you have no legal residence, principal place of business, or principal office or agency in any state:	Attn: EIN Operation Philadelphia, PA 19255 Telephone 215-516-6999 Fax-TIN 215-516-3990

How To Get Forms and Publications

Phone. You can order forms, instructions, and publications by phone 24 hours a day, 7 days a week. Call 1-800-TAX-FORM (1-800-829-3676). You should receive your order or notification of its status within 10 workdays.

Personal computer. With your personal computer and modem, you can get the forms and information you need using the IRS website at **www.irs.gov** or File Transfer Protocol at **ftp.irs.gov.**

CD-ROM. For small businesses, return preparers, or others who may frequently need tax forms or publications, a CD-ROM containing over 2,000 tax products (including many prior year forms) can be purchased from the National Technical Information Service (NTIS).

To order **Pub. 1796,** Federal Tax Products on CD-ROM, call **1-877-CDFORMS** (1-877-233-6767) toll free or connect to **www.irs.gov/cdorders.**

Tax Help for Your Business

IRS-sponsored Small Business Workshops provide information about your Federal and state tax obligations.

For information about workshops in your area, call 1-800-829-4933.

Related Forms and Publications

The following **forms** and **instructions** may be useful to filers of Form SS-4:
- **Form 990-T,** Exempt Organization Business Income Tax Return
- **Instructions for Form 990-T**
- **Schedule C (Form 1040),** Profit or Loss From Business
- **Schedule F (Form 1040),** Profit or Loss From Farming
- **Instructions for Form 1041 and Schedules A, B, D, G, I, J, and K-1,** U.S. Income Tax Return for Estates and Trusts
- **Form 1042,** Annual Withholding Tax Return for U.S. Source Income of Foreign Persons
- **Instructions for Form 1065,** U.S. Return of Partnership Income
- **Instructions for Form 1066,** U.S. Real Estate Mortgage Investment Conduit (REMIC) Income Tax Return
- **Instructions for Forms 1120 and 1120-A**
- **Form 2553,** Election by a Small Business Corporation
- **Form 2848,** Power of Attorney and Declaration of Representative
- **Form 8821,** Tax Information Authorization
- **Form 8832,** Entity Classification Election
For more **information** about filing Form SS-4 and related issues, see:
- **Circular A,** Agricultural Employer's Tax Guide (Pub. 51)
- **Circular E,** Employer's Tax Guide (Pub. 15)
- **Pub. 538,** Accounting Periods and Methods
- **Pub. 542,** Corporations
- **Pub. 557,** Exempt Status for Your Organization
- **Pub. 583,** Starting a Business and Keeping Records
- **Pub. 966,** Electronic Choices for Paying ALL Your Federal Taxes
- **Pub. 1635,** Understanding Your EIN
- **Package 1023,** Application for Recognition of Exemption Under Section 501(c)(3) of the Internal Revenue Code
- **Package 1024,** Application for Recognition of Exemption Under Section 501(a)

Specific Instructions

Print or type all entries on Form SS-4. Follow the instructions for each line to expedite processing and to avoid unnecessary IRS requests for additional information. Enter "N/A" (nonapplicable) on the lines that do not apply.

Line 1—Legal name of entity (or individual) for whom the EIN is being requested. Enter the legal name of the entity (or individual) applying for the EIN exactly as it appears on the social security card, charter, or other applicable legal document.

Individuals. Enter your first name, middle initial, and last name. If you are a sole proprietor, enter your individual name, not your business name. Enter your business name on line 2. Do not use abbreviations or nicknames on line 1.

Trusts. Enter the name of the trust.

Estate of a decedent. Enter the name of the estate.

Partnerships. Enter the legal name of the partnership as it appears in the partnership agreement.

Corporations. Enter the corporate name as it appears in the corporation charter or other legal document creating it.

Plan administrators. Enter the name of the plan administrator. A plan administrator who already has an EIN should use that number.

Line 2—Trade name of business. Enter the trade name of the business if different from the legal name. The trade name is the "doing business as " (DBA) name.

> **⚠ CAUTION** *Use the full legal name shown on line 1 on all tax returns filed for the entity. (However, if you enter a trade name on line 2 and choose to use the trade name instead of the legal name, enter the trade name on **all returns** you file.) To prevent processing delays and errors, **always** use the legal name only (or the trade name only) on **all** tax returns.*

Line 3—Executor, trustee, "care of" name. Trusts enter the name of the trustee. Estates enter the name of the executor, administrator, or other fiduciary. If the entity applying has a designated person to receive tax information, enter that person's name as the "care of" person. Enter the individual's first name, middle initial, and last name.

Lines 4a-b—Mailing address. Enter the mailing address for the entity's correspondence. If line 3 is completed, enter the address for the executor, trustee or "care of" person. Generally, this address will be used on all tax returns.

> **TIP** *File **Form 8822**, Change of Address, to report any subsequent changes to the entity's mailing address.*

Lines 5a-b—Street address. Provide the entity's physical address **only** if different from its mailing address shown in lines 4a-b. **Do not** enter a P.O. box number here.

Line 6—County and state where principal business is located. Enter the entity's primary **physical** location.

Lines 7a-b—Name of principal officer, general partner, grantor, owner, or trustor. Enter the first name, middle initial, last name, and SSN of **(a)** the principal officer if the business is a corporation, **(b)** a general partner if a partnership, **(c)** the owner of an entity that is disregarded as separate from its owner (disregarded entities owned by a corporation enter the corporation's name and EIN), or **(d)** a grantor, owner, or trustor if a trust.

If the person in question is an **alien individual** with a previously assigned individual taxpayer identification number (ITIN), enter the ITIN in the space provided and submit a copy of an official identifying document. If

necessary, complete **Form W-7**, Application for IRS Individual Taxpayer Identification Number, to obtain an ITIN.

You are **required** to enter an SSN, ITIN, or EIN unless the only reason you are applying for an EIN is to make an entity classification election (see Regulations sections 301.7701-1 through 301.7701-3) and you are a nonresident alien with no effectively connected income from sources within the United States.

Line 8a—Type of entity. Check the box that best describes the type of entity applying for the EIN. If you are an alien individual with an ITIN previously assigned to you, enter the ITIN in place of a requested SSN.

> **⚠ CAUTION** *This is not an election for a tax classification of an entity. See **Limited liability company (LLC)** on page 4.*

Other. If not specifically listed, check the "Other" box, enter the type of entity and the type of return, if any, that will be filed (for example, "Common Trust Fund, Form 1065" or "Created a Pension Plan"). Do not enter "N/A." If you are an alien individual applying for an EIN, see the **Lines 7a-b** instructions above.

● **Household employer.** If you are an individual, check the "Other" box and enter "Household Employer" and your SSN. If you are a state or local agency serving as a tax reporting agent for public assistance recipients who become household employers, check the "Other" box and enter "Household Employer Agent." If you are a trust that qualifies as a household employer, you do not need a separate EIN for reporting tax information relating to household employees; use the EIN of the trust.

● **QSub.** For a qualified subchapter S subsidiary (QSub) check the "Other" box and specify "QSub."

● **Withholding agent.** If you are a withholding agent required to file Form 1042, check the "Other" box and enter "Withholding Agent."

Sole proprietor. Check this box if you file Schedule C, C-EZ, or F (Form 1040) and have a qualified plan, or are required to file excise, employment, alcohol, tobacco, or firearms returns, or are a payer of gambling winnings. Enter your SSN (or ITIN) in the space provided. If you are a nonresident alien with no effectively connected income from sources within the United States, you do not need to enter an SSN or ITIN.

Corporation. This box is for any corporation **other than a personal service corporation.** If you check this box, enter the income tax form number to be filed by the entity in the space provided.

> **⚠ CAUTION** *If you entered "1120S" after the "Corporation" checkbox, the corporation **must** file Form 2553 **no later than the 15th day of the 3rd month of the tax year the election is to take effect.** Until Form 2553 has been received and approved, you will be considered a Form 1120 filer. See the Instructions for Form 2553.*

Personal service corp. Check this box if the entity is a personal service corporation. An entity is a personal service corporation for a tax year only if:

- The principal activity of the entity during the testing period (prior tax year) for the tax year is the performance of personal services substantially by employee-owners, and
- The employee-owners own at least 10% of the fair market value of the outstanding stock in the entity on the last day of the testing period.

Personal services include performance of services in such fields as health, law, accounting, or consulting. For more information about personal service corporations, see the Instructions for Forms 1120 and 1120-A and Pub. 542.

Other nonprofit organization. Check this box if the nonprofit organization is other than a church or church-controlled organization and specify the type of nonprofit organization (for example, an educational organization).

> ⚠ **CAUTION** *If the organization also seeks tax-exempt status, you **must** file either Package 1023 or Package 1024. See Pub. 557 for more information.*

If the organization is covered by a group exemption letter, enter the four-digit **group exemption number (GEN).** (Do not confuse the GEN with the nine-digit EIN.) If you do not know the GEN, contact the parent organization. Get Pub. 557 for more information about group exemption numbers.

Plan administrator. If the plan administrator is an individual, enter the plan administrator's SSN in the space provided.

REMIC. Check this box if the entity has elected to be treated as a real estate mortgage investment conduit (REMIC). See the Instructions for Form 1066 for more information.

Limited liability company (LLC). An LLC is an entity organized under the laws of a state or foreign country as a limited liability company. For Federal tax purposes, an LLC may be treated as a partnership or corporation or be disregarded as an entity separate from its owner.

By **default,** a domestic LLC with only one member is **disregarded** as an entity separate from its owner and must include all of its income and expenses on the owner's tax return (e.g., **Schedule C (Form 1040)**). Also by default, a domestic LLC with two or more members is treated as a partnership. A domestic LLC may file Form 8832 to avoid either default classification and elect to be classified as an association taxable as a corporation. For more information on entity classifications (including the rules for foreign entities), see the instructions for Form 8832.

> ⚠ **CAUTION** ***Do not** file Form 8832 if the LLC accepts the default classifications above. **However, if the LLC will be electing S Corporation status, it must timely file both Form 8832 and Form 2553.***

Complete Form SS-4 for LLCs as follows:
- A single-member domestic LLC that accepts the default classification (above) does not need an EIN and generally should not file Form SS-4. Generally, the LLC should use the name and EIN of its **owner** for all Federal tax purposes. However, the reporting and payment of employment taxes for employees of the LLC may be made using the name and EIN of **either** the owner or the LLC as explained in Notice 99-6. You can find Notice 99-6 on page 12 of Internal Revenue Bulletin 1999-3 at **www.irs.gov/pub/irs-irbs/irb99-03.pdf. (Note:** If the LLC applicant indicates in box 13 that it has employees or expects to have employees, the owner (whether an individual or other entity) of a single-member domestic LLC will also be assigned its own EIN (if it does not already have one) even if the LLC will be filing the employment tax returns.)
- A single-member, domestic LLC that accepts the default classification (above) and wants an EIN for filing employment tax returns (see above) or non-Federal purposes, such as a state requirement, must check the "Other" box and write "Disregarded Entity" or, when applicable, "Disregarded Entity—Sole Proprietorship" in the space provided.
- A multi-member, domestic LLC that accepts the default classification (above) must check the "Partnership" box.
- A domestic LLC that will be filing Form 8832 to elect corporate status must check the "Corporation" box and write in "Single-Member" or "Multi-Member" immediately below the "form number" entry line.

Line 9—Reason for applying. Check only **one** box. Do not enter "N/A."

Started new business. Check this box if you are starting a new business that requires an EIN. If you check this box, enter the type of business being started. **Do not** apply if you already have an EIN and are only adding another place of business.

Hired employees. Check this box if the existing business is requesting an EIN because it has hired or is hiring employees and is therefore required to file employment tax returns. **Do not** apply if you already have an EIN and are only hiring employees. For information on employment taxes (e.g., for family members), see Circular E.

> ⚠ **CAUTION** *You may be required to make electronic deposits of all depository taxes (such as employment tax, excise tax, and corporate income tax) using the Electronic Federal Tax Payment System (EFTPS). See section 11, Depositing Taxes, of Circular E and Pub. 966.*

Created a pension plan. Check this box if you have created a pension plan and need an EIN for reporting purposes. Also, enter the type of plan in the space provided.

> 💡 **TIP** *Check this box if you are applying for a trust EIN when a new pension plan is established. In addition, check the "Other" box in line 8a and write "Created a Pension Plan" in the space provided.*

Banking purpose. Check this box if you are requesting an EIN for banking purposes only, and enter the banking purpose (for example, a bowling league for depositing dues or an investment club for dividend and interest reporting).

Changed type of organization. Check this box if the business is changing its type of organization. For example, the business was a sole proprietorship and has been incorporated or has become a partnership. If you check this box, specify in the space provided (including available space immediately below) the type of change made. For example, "From Sole Proprietorship to Partnership."

Purchased going business. Check this box if you purchased an existing business. **Do not** use the former owner's EIN unless you became the "owner" of a corporation by acquiring its stock.

Created a trust. Check this box if you created a trust, and enter the type of trust created. For example, indicate if the trust is a nonexempt charitable trust or a split-interest trust.

Exception. Do **not** file this form for certain grantor-type trusts. The trustee does not need an EIN for the trust if the trustee furnishes the name and TIN of the grantor/owner and the address of the trust to all payors. See the Instructions for Form 1041 for more information.

(TIP) *Do not check this box if you are applying for a trust EIN when a new pension plan is established. Check "Created a pension plan."*

Other. Check this box if you are requesting an EIN for any other reason; and enter the reason. For example, a newly-formed state government entity should enter "Newly-Formed State Government Entity" in the space provided.

Line 10—Date business started or acquired. If you are starting a new business, enter the starting date of the business. If the business you acquired is already operating, enter the date you acquired the business. If you are changing the form of ownership of your business, enter the date the new ownership entity began. Trusts should enter the date the trust was legally created. Estates should enter the date of death of the decedent whose name appears on line 1 or the date when the estate was legally funded.

Line 11—Closing month of accounting year. Enter the last month of your accounting year or tax year. An accounting or tax year is usually 12 consecutive months, either a calendar year or a fiscal year (including a period of 52 or 53 weeks). A calendar year is 12 consecutive months ending on December 31. A fiscal year is either 12 consecutive months ending on the last day of any month other than December or a 52-53 week year. For more information on accounting periods, see Pub. 538.

Individuals. Your tax year generally will be a calendar year.

Partnerships. Partnerships must adopt one of the following tax years:
● The tax year of the majority of its partners,
● The tax year common to all of its principal partners,
● The tax year that results in the least aggregate deferral of income, or
● In certain cases, some other tax year.

See the Instructions for Form 1065 for more information.

REMICs. REMICs must have a calendar year as their tax year.

Personal service corporations. A personal service corporation generally must adopt a calendar year unless:
● It can establish a business purpose for having a different tax year, or
● It elects under section 444 to have a tax year other than a calendar year.

Trusts. Generally, a trust must adopt a calendar year except for the following:
● Tax-exempt trusts,
● Charitable trusts, and
● Grantor-owned trusts.

Line 12—First date wages or annuities were paid or will be paid. If the business has or will have employees, enter the date on which the business began or will begin to pay wages. If the business does not plan to have employees, enter "N/A."

Withholding agent. Enter the date you began or will begin to pay income (including annuities) to a nonresident alien. This also applies to individuals who are required to file Form 1042 to report alimony paid to a nonresident alien.

Line 13—Highest number of employees expected in the next 12 months. Complete each box by entering the number (including zero ("-0-")) of "Agricultural," "Household," or "Other" employees expected by the applicant in the next 12 months. For a definition of agricultural labor (farmwork), see Circular A.

Lines 14 and 15. Check the **one** box in line 14 that best describes the principal activity of the applicant's business. Check the "Other" box (and specify the applicant's principal activity) if none of the listed boxes applies.

Use line 15 to describe the applicant's principal line of business in more detail. For example, if you checked the "Construction" box in line 14, enter additional detail such as "General contractor for residential buildings" in line 15.

Construction. Check this box if the applicant is engaged in erecting buildings or other structures, (e.g., streets, highways, bridges, tunnels). The term "Construction" also includes special trade contractors, (e.g., plumbing, HVAC, electrical, carpentry, concrete, excavation, etc. contractors).

Real estate. Check this box if the applicant is engaged in renting or leasing real estate to others; managing, selling, buying or renting real estate for others; or providing related real estate services (e.g., appraisal services).

Rental and leasing. Check this box if the applicant is engaged in providing tangible goods such as autos, computers, consumer goods, or industrial machinery and equipment to customers in return for a periodic rental or lease payment.

Manufacturing. Check this box if the applicant is engaged in the mechanical, physical, or chemical transformation of materials, substances, or components into new products. The assembling of component parts of manufactured products is also considered to be manufacturing.

Transportation & warehousing. Check this box if the applicant provides transportation of passengers or cargo; warehousing or storage of goods; scenic or sight-seeing transportation; or support activities related to these modes of transportation.

Finance & insurance. Check this box if the applicant is engaged in transactions involving the creation, liquidation, or change of ownership of financial assets and/or facilitating such financial transactions; underwriting annuities/insurance policies; facilitating such underwriting by selling insurance policies; or by providing other insurance or employee-benefit related services.

Health care and social assistance. Check this box if the applicant is engaged in providing physical, medical, or psychiatric care using licensed health care professionals or providing social assistance activities such as youth centers, adoption agencies, individual/family services, temporary shelters, etc.

Accommodation & food services. Check this box if the applicant is engaged in providing customers with lodging, meal preparation, snacks, or beverages for immediate consumption.

Wholesale–agent/broker. Check this box if the applicant is engaged in arranging for the purchase or sale of goods owned by others or purchasing goods on a commission basis for goods traded in the wholesale market, usually between businesses.

Wholesale–other. Check this box if the applicant is engaged in selling goods in the wholesale market generally to other businesses for resale on their own account.

Retail. Check this box if the applicant is engaged in selling merchandise to the general public from a fixed store; by direct, mail-order, or electronic sales; or by using vending machines.

Other. Check this box if the applicant is engaged in an activity not described above. Describe the applicant's principal business activity in the space provided.

Lines 16a-c. Check the applicable box in line 16a to indicate whether or not the entity (or individual) applying for an EIN was issued one previously. Complete lines 16b and 16c **only** if the "Yes" box in line 16a is checked. If the applicant previously applied for **more than one** EIN, write "See Attached" in the empty space in line 16a and attach a separate sheet providing the line 16b and 16c information for each EIN previously requested.

Third Party Designee. Complete this section **only** if you want to authorize the named individual to receive the entity's EIN and answer questions about the completion of Form SS-4. The designee's authority terminates at the time the EIN is assigned and released to the designee. **You must complete the signature area for the authorization to be valid.**

Signature. When required, the application must be signed by **(a)** the individual, if the applicant is an individual, **(b)** the president, vice president, or other principal officer, if the applicant is a corporation, **(c)** a responsible and duly authorized member or officer having knowledge of its affairs, if the applicant is a partnership, government entity, or other unincorporated organization, or **(d)** the fiduciary, if the applicant is a trust or an estate. Foreign applicants may have any duly-authorized person, (e.g., division manager), sign Form SS-4.

Privacy Act and Paperwork Reduction Act Notice. We ask for the information on this form to carry out the Internal Revenue laws of the United States. We need it to comply with section 6109 and the regulations thereunder which generally require the inclusion of an employer identification number (EIN) on certain returns, statements, or other documents filed with the Internal Revenue Service. If your entity is required to obtain an EIN, you are required to provide all of the information requested on this form. Information on this form may be used to determine which Federal tax returns you are required to file and to provide you with related forms and publications.

We disclose this form to the Social Security Administration for their use in determining compliance with applicable laws. We may give this information to the Department of Justice for use in civil and criminal litigation, and to the cities, states, and the District of Columbia for use in administering their tax laws. We may also disclose this information to Federal and state agencies to enforce Federal nontax criminal laws and to combat terrorism.

We will be unable to issue an EIN to you unless you provide all of the requested information which applies to your entity. Providing false information could subject you to penalties.

You are not required to provide the information requested on a form that is subject to the Paperwork Reduction Act unless the form displays a valid OMB control number. Books or records relating to a form or its instructions must be retained as long as their contents may become material in the administration of any Internal Revenue law. Generally, tax returns and return information are confidential, as required by section 6103.

The time needed to complete and file this form will vary depending on individual circumstances. The estimated average time is:

Recordkeeping	6 min.
Learning about the law or the form	22 min.
Preparing the form	46 min.
Copying, assembling, and sending the form to the IRS	20 min.

If you have comments concerning the accuracy of these time estimates or suggestions for making this form simpler, we would be happy to hear from you. You can write to the Tax Products Coordinating Committee, Western Area Distribution Center, Rancho Cordova, CA 95743-0001. **Do not** send the form to this address. Instead, see **How To Apply** on page 1.

Printed on recycled paper

GRANT WRITING AND NON-PROFIT DEVELOPMENT CHECKLIST

Grant writing is only one component of developing a sustainable non-profit organization. This checklist is not exhaustive but very close. Follow these guidelines and refer to the agencies listed at the end of the section to learn how to form and develop your non-profit as well as secure grant funding.

Item	Date	Who's Responsible	Status	Note
Preparation is Never Lost Time (Organizational Structure and Program Development)				
Develop a Strategic Plan and/or Business Plan with goals for 5, 10, 15, 20 years using *Visions International's* The Visioning Process™				
Build your team				
Get team approval and assign roles and responsibilities				
Assess your organizational capacity – human, financial, service and product resources				
Establish files, bios and resumes on all personnel, staff and board members				
Share copies of previous grants submitted				
Develop a Planning Calendar of deadlines for proposals, grant development, grant writing cycles, meetings, fundraising, public relations events, etc.				
Gather documentation of non-profit/legal status - articles of incorporation, tax exemption certificates, and bylaws				
Gather budgets, tax returns, financial statements, etc. for past 3 to 5 years				
Gather documentation of your organization's involvement in your targeted community, evidence of collaboration, and progress				
Gather awards and recognitions, news clippings, program information, photos				
Attend grant writing, program development workshops				
Compile a wish list of goods, services, materials including present inventory list				

GRANT WRITING AND NON-PROFIT DEVELOPMENT CHECKLIST

Item	Date	Who's Responsible	Status	Note
After You Pick up the Ball but Before You Start Running (The Potential Grantor and Supporters)				
Be sure there is not a duplication of your program/efforts by contacting legislators, area government agencies and related public and private agencies. Are there significant differences and improvements?				
Once your proposal summary is developed, seek support from individuals or groups representing academic, political, community, professional, and religious organizations				
Get letters of endorsement detailing exact areas of project support and commitment				
If required, affiliation agreements to share services between agencies and building space				
Are you/program an acceptable candidate for funding? Do you and the grantor have the same interests, intentions, and needs?				
Identify a potential grantor				
Contact the grantor, request a grant application kit				
Distribute copies of grant application and forms and grantor contact info to team				
Become familiar with all pertinent program/grant criteria				

GRANT WRITING AND NON-PROFIT DEVELOPMENT CHECKLIST ⬤⬤⬤⬤⬤⬤

Item	Date	Who's Responsible	Status	Note
After You Pick up the Ball but Before You Start Running (The Potential Grantor and Supporters)				
Later, get to know some of the grantor agency personnel. Ask for suggestions, criticisms, and advice about the proposed project.				
Send the proposal summary to a specific agency official with a separate cover letter, and ask for review and comment?				
Make a personal visit to the agency's regional office or headquarters - establish face-to-face contact, get essential details about the proposal, secure literature and references from the agency's library.				
Reviewing the federal budget for the current and budget fiscal years to determine proposed dollars for particular budget functions.				
Review eligibility requirements				
Start · Begin · Pick up the Pieces · Stay on Target (Needs Assessment/Supporting Data)				
Organize and keep all your ideas				
Establish files of statistics on the population you serve - historical, geographic, quantitative, factual, statistical, and philosophical, studies and literature searches.				
Collect local data				
Collect state data				
Collect national data				
Do a data comparison				
Develop a method to survey the needs				
Mail the survey				
Follow-up on the survey				
Compile survey results				
Facilitate a needs assessment meeting(s)				
Compile final results of needs assessment from surveys and meetings.				

GRANT WRITING AND NON-PROFIT DEVELOPMENT CHECKLIST

Item	Date	Who's Responsible	Status	Note
Develop a Proposal as to Get the Approval (Proposal Development)				
Determine the required components of the proposal. The eight basic components to creating a solid proposal package: (1) the proposal summary (2) introduction of organization (3) the problem statement (or needs assessment) (4) project objectives (5) project methods or design (6) project evaluation (7) future funding/sustainability (8) project budget.				
Write (1) the proposal summary				
Write (2) introduction of organization				
Write (3) the problem statement (or needs assessment)				
Write (4) project goals and objectives				
Write (5) project methods or design				
Write (6) project evaluation				
Write (7) future funding/sustainability plan				
Determine (8) overall project budget/categories				
Calculate all travel				
Calculate all lodging				
Calculate personnel costs for program director, coordinator, consultants, other staff				
Calculate subcontract labor				
Calculate stipends				
Calculate indirect costs				
Calculate utilities				
Determine match funds or in-kind contributions				
Calculate special program needs				
Compile budget detail				
Write budget justification and a narrative consistent with the budget				

GRANT WRITING AND NON-PROFIT DEVELOPMENT CHECKLIST ●●●●●●

Item	Date	Who's Responsible	Status	Note
Develop a Proposal as to Get the Approval (Proposal Development)				
Develop a timeline (brief of overall Planning Calendar)				
Organize the Appendices (i.e. time tables, work plans, schedules, activities, methodologies, legal papers, personnel vitae, letters of support, and endorsements)				
Write Table of Contents				
Write the Abstract				
Edit and revise				
Review to be sure your proposal addresses all requirements of the grant				
Copy and distribute the proposal for an internal review				
Do an external review				
Revise based on the reviews				
Sign the assurances, agreements and application				
Make copies for the team, partners, and grantor (if required)				
Distribute copies and thank you notes/letters				
Submit proposal by the deadline; nothing more and nothing less than what was requested				
Send the application certified mail with return receipt				
Spread the Word (Marketing and Public Relations)				
After you have been awarded the grant, do a press release				
Reach your targeted community				
Reserve an internet domain name for a website				
Develop brochures, flyers, etc.				

GRANT WRITING AND NON-PROFIT DEVELOPMENT CHECKLIST

Item	Date	Who's Responsible	Status	Note
Keep Your Funding and Support! (Accountability, Evaluation and Improvements)				
Be proactive towards growth and change by actually using and updating your Strategic Plan				
Revise your plan as needed				
Implement necessary program improvements				
Hold timely (monthly, quarterly) planning/strategy meetings				
Actually implement what you said you were going to do in your grant proposal				
Conceptualize your program by creating a diagram of Program/Method/Actions/Results (i.e. Make four columns: (1) Program Details/Description – "Tutoring" (2) Method – "Hire 3 tutors" (3) Actions – "Tutor, keep progress reports" (4) Results – "15 Children tutored and each child's improvements"				
Implement a Program Evaluation and Review Technique. Do an internal, external evaluation or both based on (1) product evaluation - results of the project and satisfaction of its desired objectives (2) process evaluation - how the project was conducted - consistency with the stated plan the effectiveness of the activities within the plan				
Exercise fiscal accountability; hire an external accountant if necessary				
Form a development team that focuses on funding and sustainability				
Establish an on-going funding cycle for other submissions				

EXAMINING A REQUEST FOR PROPOSAL (RFP)

1. Who is eligible to apply?
2. When is the deadline? In-hand deadline or post-marked deadline?
3. What type of programs or activities does the grant support? Is the grantor's goal consistent with the strategic goals of your organization? Is their target market your target market?
4. What type of partners or collaboration are they looking for?
5. Scan the RFP for keywords and repetitive words/phrases, highlight these?
6. How do they "define" certain aspects of the program? (i.e. personnel, program income)
7. Are there any restrictions?
8. What are the main criteria/key information the reviewers will be use to review and evaluate your proposal?
9. What are the point values assigned to each criteria?
10. Are there any competitive points to be gained? If so, can you meet the requirement to gain them?
11. Is there a match funding or in-kind requirement?
12. Can it be a new or existing program?
13. What is the grant amount?
14. How much can your request? Can you apply for less than the grant amount?
15. What is the grant period?
16. Who is the contact person for the grantor?
17. Do they provide any technical assistance training workshops to prepare your grant application?
18. Do you have to submit a preliminary letter?
19. Is the application available on-line?
20. Do you have to use there forms? (i.e. budget)
21. Are past awarded grants available for review?
22. What are the technical writing requirements? (i.e. font, font size, margins, page numbers, spacing, etc.)
23. Who has to sign the application and how many signatures are required?
24. What can and can not be submitted in your appendices?
25. How many copies do you have to submit?
26. How should it be packaged?

COMMON QUESTIONS GRANT REVIEWERS ASK ABOUT PROPOSALS

(Adapted from Getting the Most Out of Your Project and Proposal: A Guide From Beginning to End, by Jamie Levy (J.D. Levy and Associates, 1998). www.fastennetwork.org)

- Does this project fit funding guidelines and funding areas?
- What is the importance of this project?
- Who is affected by this project?
- Is this project realistic?
- Are the project goals and objectives realistic?
- Can the timeline be met?
- Is the submitting organization capable committed to the project?
- Is the submitting organization capable of carrying out the project?
- Does this project duplicate others in the field?
- If there is duplication, why is this project stronger?
- Is the staff of the organization capable and accountable?
- Is the cost of this project justified and realistic?
- What is the history of the organization; has it shown success?
- Will this project be continued when the money is gone?
- Is there collaboration involved in the project?
- Do the submitters have external support?
- Is this an all-or-none type of project, or can we choose to fund portions of it?
- Is this a solid investment for our organization or another?
- Is the submitting organization able to receive a grant?
- Does the submitting organization need help in further developing the idea or has it been done well?
- Are there any overlooked aspects of the project that the submitting organization should be made aware of?

GRANT WRITING AND NON-PROFIT DIRECTORY

The following is a directory of organizations that provide products and services in grant and non-profit development. Visions International does not endorse or guarantee the products or services of these organizations.

Research Associates
www.grantexperts.com
A university-affiliated organization providing a variety of grant development services and products.
169 Laurelhurst Avenue
Columbia, SC 29210-3825
803.750.9759

FASTEN
www.fastennetwork.org
FASTEN offers networking opportunities and informational resources to equip faith-based practitioners, private philanthropists, and public administrators seeking to collaborate effectively to renew urban communities.

The Foundation Center
http://fdncenter.org/
The Foundation Center's mission is to strengthen the nonprofit sector by advancing knowledge about U.S. philanthropy. To achieve our mission, we collect, organize, and communicate information on U.S. philanthropy, conduct and facilitate research on trends in the field and provide education and training on the grant seeking process.

Ensure public access to information and services through our web site, print and electronic publications, five library/learning centers, and a national network of Cooperating Collections.

U.S. Small Business Administration (SBA) Federal and State Grant Resources
http://sba.gov/expanding/grants.html

The U.S. Small Business Administration does not offer grants to start or expand small businesses, although it does offer a wide variety of loan programs. (See http://www.sba.gov/financing for more information) While SBA does offer some grant programs, these are generally designed to expand and enhance organizations that provide small business management, technical, or financial assistance. These grants generally support non-profit organizations, intermediary lending institutions, and state and local governments. (See Federal and State Technology Partnership Program, Women's Business Center Program Announcements and visit New Markets Venture Capital Program.)

Department of Health and Human Services (HHS)
http://www.acf.hhs.gov/acf_about.html
The Administration for Children and Families (ACF), within the Department of Health and Human Services (HHS) is responsible for federal programs that promote the economic and social well-being of families, children, individuals, and communities. ACF programs aim to achieve the following:

- families and individuals empowered to increase their own economic independence and productivity;
- strong, healthy, supportive communities that have a positive impact on the quality of life and the development of children;
- partnerships with individuals, front-line service providers, communities, American Indian tribes, Native communities, states, and Congress that enable solutions which transcend traditional agency boundaries;
- services planned, reformed, and integrated to improve needed access;
- and a strong commitment to working with people with developmental disabilities, refugees, and migrants to address their needs, strengths, and abilities.

Afterschool.gov
http://www.afterschool.gov
Afterschool.gov offers one-stop access to government resources that support after school programs. The site is designed for anyone who cares about kids 6-18-providers, parents, and kids and teens. You can find information to help you understand the issues that face kids and teens or fund, start and operate an after school program. You don't even need to know which Federal agency has the information you need-- afterschool.gov searched the sites for the information requested most often and put it in easy to use categories. Research studies, news and publications are added as they are released to keep you up to date on what is happening in the field of after school programs.

Environmental Protection Agency (EPA) Grant Writing Tutorial
http://www.epa.gov/grtlakes/seahome/grants.html
This interactive software tool walks the user through the grant-writing process and helps them learn to write more competitive grants. The program includes:

- detailed information and tips on writing a grant proposal;
- how to complete a grant application package;
- program-specific sections on three EPA grant programs:
- Environmental Justice
- Environmental Justice Through Pollution Prevention
- Environmental Education
- examples of good, complete grant packages;
- references;
- a glossary of terms;
- resources and contacts;
- a mock grant-writing activity where the user is able to compare their results to a successful grant application

Grants.gov
www.grants.gov
Grants.gov allows organizations to electronically find and apply for competitive grant opportunities from all Federal grant-making agencies. Grants.gov is THE single access point for over 900 grant programs offered by the 26 Federal grant-making agencies. The US Department of Health and Human Services is proud to be the managing partner for Grants.gov, an initiative that will have an unparalleled impact on the grant community.

The Grantsmanship Center Library of Winning Proposals
http://www.tgcigrantproposals.com/
The proposals provide a wealth of useful information, examples, and insights. Your organizations can use these top-ranked grant proposals as
- Examples of effective grant proposal writing
- Models for designing cutting-edge programs
- Examples of today's best practices in your field
- Illustrations of how to construct a program budget

Associated Grant Makers
http://www.agmconnect.org/
AGM's mission is to support the practice and expansion of effective philanthropic giving. AGM's members are among the most highly skilled and best informed philanthropists in the country.
Go to the following sites to see a list of grant makers accept these forms.
Common Proposal Form: http://www.agmconnect.org/GrantSeekers/cpf.htm
Common Report Form: http://www.agmconnect.org/GrantSeekers/crf.htm

Non-profit Good Practice Guide
http://www.npgoodpractice.org/
The Nonprofit Good Practice Guide is a one-stop shop for widely-accepted and innovative nonprofit practices offering Preferred Practices and Pitfalls, Glossaries, Resources, Trends and Web site Profiles within ten topic areas.

Basic Guide to Non-Profit Financial Management
http://www.mapnp.org/library/finance/np_fnce/np_fnce.htm#anchor1786028

Fundraiser Software
http://www.fundraiser-software.com/
FundRaiser Software is designed to meet the needs of nonprofit organizations of all sizes.

Raising More Money
http://www.raisingmoremoney.com
Raising More Money trains and coaches nonprofit organizations to implement a mission-based system for raising sustainable funding from individual donors.

AGM Common Proposal Form

Before writing your proposal using the AGM Common Proposal Form, please read this page carefully. These tips and suggestions are written with you, the writer, in mind.

When writing a proposal, make sure that the goals, objectives, and amount requested match the criteria of the funder you are approaching. Be strategic!

Understanding that many foundations have small staff sizes, calling a foundation or corporate giving program to seek their advice if you do have a concern about a particular question may be useful.

Do Your Homework!
Keep these following tips in mind:

1. Research each funder's grant making philosophy, program interests, and criteria.
2. Be aware of each funder's application process, including timetable and preferred method of initial contact.
3. Include a cover letter, introducing your organization and stating the dollar request.
   (Check with each funder to see if they have a separate cover sheet.)
4. Follow any specific instructions from the funder.

There are many resources to help you in your research. Utilize them! Following are some suggestions:

- Call or write each funder to obtain a copy of its funding guidelines

- Use *Associated Grant Makers Directory*, profiling nearly 500 funding organizations

- Use National Directories and databases

- Visit AGM's Resource Center for Philanthropy in New England's premiere funding research library

- Join AGM's Partners Program and receive publications of the *Partners Update*, invitations to meeting and program, discounts on registration fees and library purchases

- Utilize AGMConnect found at *www.agmconnect.org*

Associated Grant Makers (AGM) is a regional association of corporate and foundation grant makers. AGM's mission is to support the practice and expansion of effective philanthropic giving.

AGM DOES NOT MAKE GRANTS. PLEASE DO NOT SEND FUNDING REQUESTS TO AGM.

Feel free to share the Common Proposal Form with a nonprofit colleague!

Cover Summary

Date: _____

1. Legal name of organization, address, and name of executive director:

2. IRS 501(c)(3) nonprofit? (Please circle)   YES   NO

    2a. If no, identify your fiscal agent and attach the written agreement from the fiscal agent. (Funders using this form may have special requirements as to the use of a fiscal agent, or may not permit such use.)

3. Contact person and title: _____

4. Phone: _____ FAX: _____ Email: _____

5. AMOUNT REQUESTED: $_____

6. TYPE OF REQUEST (operating, project, capital, other): _____

7. State your organization's mission:

8. No more than four sentences summarizing the proposal and its strategic link with this funder (Include the name of the project or capital campaign, if applicable):

9. List the proposal's target population, constituents, and geographic communities:

10. Total number of board members: _____ Total number of volunteers: _____

11. Total number of staff: Full-time _____ Part-time _____

12. Total annual organizational budget: $_____ Fiscal Year End ___/___/___

13. Project or capital budget (if applicable): $_____

14. The period this grant will cover: ___/___ to ___/___

15. United Way affiliate? (Please circle): YES NO

16. List any previous support from this funder in the last five years.

Proposal Narrative

Up to 10 pages is *suggested*. Check to see that the goals, objectives, and amount requested in your proposal match the criteria of the funder you are approaching. The following questions are ones that funders have identified as important information to answer. **While it is necessary to encompass all the following information in the proposal narrative, you may want to change the order in which you answer these questions.**

Profile of your organization and of your request
- *If you are requesting operating support, please provide information about your organization's overall programs and activities.*
- *If you are requesting project or capital support, please provide information for that specific project or capital request.*

1. Brief summary of organization's history, goals, and key achievements.
2. Overview of organization's structure and programs, including board, staff, and volunteer involvement.
3. Describe your organization's constituents for the organization overall, or, for a specific project. For example, total number and breakdown by age, gender, race/ethnicity, income levels, disabilities, geography, language spoken, or other criteria relevant to your organization or project.
4. Describe the community or regional need(s) and/or challenges that this effort will address. What is the level and nature of involvement of the community-at-large?
5. Description of the specific request that includes goals and objectives. (If it's a project request, provide a profile of the project)
6. Specific activities and timetable for meeting your stated objectives.
7. Future plan for sustaining this effort and strategy for building your funding base.
8. Who are your staff and volunteers and what are their qualifications?
9. If applicable, identify organizations that you collaborate with to address the issue(s) in this proposal.

Evaluation
10. Define your criteria for success for the organization, project, or capital campaign. State how you will measure your success in the short-term and in the long-term. What tool(s) will be used to evaluate your program or organization? What is your strategy for implementing the evaluation process?

Remember ⇒ Refer to each funder's guidelines to see if additional information is required

Attachments
All of the following attachments must accompany the proposal
1. IRS letter confirming tax-exempt status - 501(c)(3) and 509(a).
2. Current board list with relevant background, affiliations, town residence, and number of times a year it meets
3. Financial information:
- Total board approved organizational budget for the fiscal year(s) (see page 4 for details)
- If seeking project or capital support, include project or capital budget for fiscal year(s)
- Most recent independent audit or account review (as required by law)*
- Year-to-date financial statement for the current fiscal year
- List companies and foundations being approached to fund this proposal, with dollar amounts indicating which sources are committed, pending, or anticipated

Important ⇒ Refer to each funder's guidelines to see if additional attachments, such as diversity forms, IRS Form 990, or resumes are required.

*Footnote: according to the Massachusetts Attorney General's Division of Public Charities, nonprofits with revenues of equal to or more than $250,000 must conduct an annual independent audit. Those with revenues between $100,000 and $249,999 may conduct an account review in lieu of an independent audit. Any nonprofit with revenues of $99,999 or less is not required to conduct an independent audit or an account review. For more information, call the Massachusetts Attorney General's Office at 617.727.2200.

Proposal Budget/Budget Narrative

2 PAGES MAXIMUM

Before You Begin! Important Note:
If you already prepare organizational, project, or capital budgets which include revenues and expenses, you may submit them in their original form, or use the following sample.

1. Time period budget covers:

2. Revenue: provide a line item revenue statement for all applicable budget categories.
   a. Grants and Contracts
      - Local Government
      - State Government
      - Federal Government
      - Foundations and Corporations
      - United Way and Other Federated Campaigns

   b. Other Fundraising and Earned Income
      - Individuals
      - Events

   c. Earned Income
      - Publications and Products
      - Membership Income
      - Fees

3. Expenses: provide a line item expense budget, with narrative footnotes for those applicable items which need further explanation. Typical line items might include:
   - Salaries (specify number of full time equivalents)
   - Payroll Taxes
   - Fringe Benefits
   - Consultants and Professional Fees
   - Insurance
   - Travel/Transportation
   - Equipment
   - Supplies
   - Printing and Copying
   - Telephone and Fax
   - Postage and Delivery
   - Rent
   - Utilities
   - Maintenance
   - Evaluation
   - Staff Development and Training
   - Child Care
   - Administrative Overhead

4. In-Kind Support

AGM Common Report Form

Check One: ☐ Interim Report (Submit only this cover sheet)
☐ Final Report (Submit this cover sheet and complete page 2 using no more than three pages.)

Submitted to: _____   Date: _____

Name of Organization:
_____
Fiscal Agent (if different from your organization): _____
Address:
_____
_____

Phone: _____ Fax: _____ Email:
_____
Contact person: _____
Title: _____
Program Name (if applicable):
_____
Grant Amount: _____
☐ General Operating   ☐ Project Support   ☐ Challenge Grant   ☐ Capital/Endowment
Period that this report covers: ___/___ to ___/___

Please provide a complete expense report indicating how the grant award was used. **If this is an Interim Report**, please indicate expenses to date.

Complete the following two questions ONLY if this is an Interim Report.

1. List up to five accomplishments or progress towards meeting your goals and objectives so far.

2. Have there been any delays in meeting objectives? If so, please explain them.

Please respond to each of the following questions using up to 3 (three) pages in total, not including the cover page. Your responses should focus specifically on the funded project or program, if applicable, or in the case of general operating grants, on your entire organization.

1. Referring to the goals and objectives described in your original grant request (or any revisions submitted subsequent to the grant award), please indicate the following:
   a. What were your major accomplishments?
   b. What steps or actions were used to meet your objectives and goals?
   c. What measures were used to determine your progress?
   d. What were the unexpected results or key learnings you would share with funders?

2. Describe any setbacks encountered during the period of this grant.
   a. How did these setbacks impact your organization or project?
   b. How were these setbacks addressed?

3. Who else has funded this project (or your organization), and at what level? If total proposed budget amount was not raised, indicate if program goals were altered in any way.

4. What steps are being made to ensure the sustainability of your project or organization beyond this grant period?

5. If your program involved collaboration with other organizations, please comment on its effect upon the program.

Check with individual funders about their requirements or additional attachments:
_____ Promotional/dissemination materials (i.e. brochures, flyers, ad copy)
_____ News clippings
_____ List of current Board of Directors
_____ Most recent audit, account review, or end of year financial statement

**FINAL REPORTS MUST BE SUBMITTED NO LATER THAN SIXTY DAYS
AFTER THE END OF THE GRANT PERIOD, OR
WITHIN THE TIME SPECIFIED BY EACH FUNDER.**

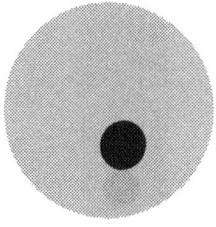

APPENDIX

A

FEDERAL AND STATE REGULATIONS

Every small business is subject to some state, local, and federal regulations. The following is a list of some of the most common requirements for small businesses. This list is not comprehensive so be sure to investigate state, local, and industry regulations specific to your business. If you are in the food service business, you will have to deal with the health department. If you use chemical solvents, you will have environmental compliance to meet. Not complying with established regulations can leave you with hefty penalties legally and financially.

Business License

There are many types of licenses. License fees vary by type of business and are based on sales revenues. If the business is located within an incorporated city limits, a license must be obtained from the city; if outside the city limits, then from the county. A license must also be obtained in every municipality in which you conduct business. For more information contact the city hall or county office in your area.

Special License

Certain professions and businesses require additional licenses and examinations. Contact the Department of Consumer Affairs to learn about special licenses that may be required for your business.

Contractors and Residential Builders License

Contact:

Department of Labor, License and Registration

Certificate of Occupancy

If you are planning on occupying a new or used building for a new business, you may have to apply for a Certificate of Occupancy from the local Business Inspections Department. A building inspector and fire inspector will also come out to perform an inspection. Some home-based businesses also need an occupancy permit. For more information contact the county or city office in your area.

Building and Zoning

Before you locate a business inside or outside your home check your local zoning ordinances. Contact your local county office.

Construction on a Building for Business

A Construction Certificate of Occupancy is required which is different from a Certificate of Occupancy.

Signage

Signs are also subject to approval by local zoning and building inspections divisions. The city may also charge a license fee for your sign.

FEDERAL AND STATE REGULATIONS ●●●●●●●

Health Department

If you are in the food service business, contact your county health department to obtain proper permits and licenses.

Restaurants

If your building is new or has never been a restaurant before, you must submit a seating layout to building inspections for Certificate of Occupancy approval. If your restaurant is a change of ownership or existing restaurant you may contact your local Department of Health and Environmental Control, the Division of Food Protection.

Obtaining a Bar Code or Universal Product Code (UPC)

- Go to the Uniform Code Counsel website to obtain an application for a bar code.
- The fee is based on annual sales. However, there is a minimum fee for new products.
- Processing the application takes 10 – 15 business days upon receipt of the application and fee.
- You will be issued a bar code and instructions for getting it on your product.

Uniform Code Counsel
Post Office Box 1244
Dayton, Ohio 45401
937.435.3870
www.uc-counsel.org

Census Data

The State Data Center can provide assistance and census data on population estimates and projections, sources of date, census concepts and definitions, and interpretation and use of data. Contact your State Data Center, Division of Research and Statistical Services

Fictitious Business Name

Businesses that use a name other than the owner's name must register the fictitious name with the county. This does not apply to corporations doing business under their corporate name or to those practicing any profession under a partnership name. For more information contact your local clerk of court or state government.

Check to see if your business name is available by conducting a search through the Secretary of State's office and by looking in your local county Clerk of Court's Office Mercantile Establishments Book where all business names are registered.

Legal Advice

To locate an attorney in your area or one with expertise in special areas, contact your states Bar Association. There may even be a Lawyer Referral Service.

Real Estate

Be very careful about real estate transactions. Before signing a lease or contract speak with an attorney. Your state may have an Association of Realtors to contact.

State Registration of a Trademark

Trademarks and service marks may be registered in a state for a specific term. For more information about Applications for Registration of Trademark or Service Mark in your state, contact the Secretary of State's office.

Federal Registration of Trademark and Patent

To register a trademark contact:

U.S. Department of Commerce
Trademark Office
2021 Jefferson Davis Highway
Arlington, Virginia 22202
703.305.8341 or 1.800.786.9199

To register a patent, contact:

Asst. Commissioner for Trademarks,
Patent Applications
Washington, D.C. 20231
1.800.786.9199
www.uspto.gov

Caution: Federally registered trademarks may conflict with and supersede state registered business and product names. Businesses are encouraged to check for conflicts with federal trademarks.

Patents

Contact:

Superintendent of Documents
P.O. Box 371954
Pittsburgh, Pennsylvania 15250-7954
412.512.1800

New and useful inventions can be protected by a U.S. patent. Professional assistance from a patent attorney is strongly urged because patent procedures are detailed and technical. A patent search is performed to see if a patent currently exists on the same or nearly the same device and, if not, to make proper application with the Patent Office. Information on patent laws and inventions is available through federal bookstores and the Department of Commerce.

Note: Only attorneys and agents registered with the U.S. Patent Office may represent inventors in related matters. The office has geographical and alphabetical listings of the more than 11,000 registered agents. Only these agents may perform patent searches in the patent office. Inventors or their attorneys can make arrangements with one of those agents. U.S. patents are issued by the Assistant Commissioner of Patents, Washington, D.C.

Additional information is provided in the publication, "General Information Concerning Patents" and other publications distributed through the U.S. Patent and Trademark Office.

Copyrights

Contact:

U.S. Library of Congress
James Madison Memorial Building
Washington, D.C. 20559
202.707.9100 - Order Line
202.707.3000 - Information Line

Copyrights protect the thoughts and ideas of authors, composers and artists. A copyright prevents illegal copying of written matter, works of art or computer programs. In order to ensure copyright protection, the copyright owner should always include notices on all copies of the work.

Tax Information

Business owners are typically responsible for three types of federal collections and payments: Income tax withheld from employees' wages (proprietorships, partnerships, and corporations with employees are required to file federal tax reports), FICA (Social Security) Insurance, and FUTA (Federal Unemployment Tax).

Income taxes will also be levied by the federal and state governments on earnings of any business. Therefore, each business must file an income tax return with both agencies. Businesses may be required to file estimated tax returns and pay estimated taxes on a quarterly basis.

Your federal tax ID number (TIN or EIN) can be obtained by completing and submitting IRS Form SS4 (owner's social security number may be used for sole proprietorships with no employees).

For federal tax information or to obtain your Tax ID, contact:

U.S. Internal Revenue Service (IRS)
Phone 1.866.816.2065
Fax   631.447.8960
www.irs.gov

You can go to IRS's website area for business taxes or call your local IRS office to receive a number of publications that are available upon request to small businesses. One of the most helpful is "Your Business Tax Kit", which includes data and forms for a Federal Employer Identification Number and a tax guide for small businesses that can be ordered by calling Forms and Publications at 1.800.829.3676 or through a visit to your local IRS office.

You may want to contact your local Social Security Administration Office for (FICA) Insurance information www.ssa.gov

For State tax information, try your state's web sites for tax information, call your state government or visit your official state Web site.

The IRS also offers local IRS Small Business Tax Workshops. For more information and reservations, contact your local SBDC (Small Business Development Center).

The IRS even offers state specific Business Tax Guides.

Contact:

State Department of Revenue

Property Tax

If you are a manufacturer and your business owns real property, check with you county Tax Assessor's Office to find out about property tax. You may also be liable for state property taxes on equipment and inventory. For more information contact:

Department of Revenue
State Property Tax Division

Federal Self-Employment Tax

Everyone must pay Social Security Tax. If you are self-employed, your Social Security contribution is made through the self-employment tax. You will need to calculate how best to report earnings and pay your business taxes.

Contact the IRS at 800.829.1040, visit your local IRS office, go to the Official IRS Web site for more information. The IRS may seem like a complicated maze, but there are publications, counselors and workshops available to help you sort it out.

Employee Recruitment

Job Service at your local Employment Security Commission helps employers locate and train employees or assist business owners in solving employee problems such as absenteeism and turnover.

Employment Security Commission

Business Insurance

Business insurance shields your assets and earnings against fire, theft and other losses or risks. Contact your insurance agent or broker. Insurance agents can be found in the Yellow Pages or contact your state's Department of Insurance.

Business Insurance

It is wise for any business to purchase a number of basic types of insurance. Some types of coverage are required by law, other simply make good business sense. The types of insurance listed below are among the most commonly used and are merely a starting point for evaluating the needs of your business.

- Liability Insurance -- Businesses may incur various forms of liability in conducting their normal activities. One of the most common types is product liability, which may be incurred when a customer suffers harm from using the business product. There are many other types of liability, which are frequently related to specific industries. Liability law is constantly changing. An analysis of your liability insurance needs by a competent professional is vital in determining an adequate and appropriate level of protection for your business.

- Property -- There are many different types of property insurance and levels of coverage available. It is important to determine the property you need to insure for the continuation of your business and the level of insurance you need to replace or rebuild. You must also understand the terms of the insurance, including any limitations or waivers of coverage.

- Business Interruption -- While property insurance may pay enough to replace damaged or destroyed equipment or buildings, how will you pay costs such as taxes, utilities and other continuing expenses during the period between when the damage occurs and when the property is replaced? Business Interruption (or "business income") insurance can provide sufficient funds to pay your fixed expenses during a period of time when your business is not operational.

- "Key Man" -- If you (and/or any other individual) are so critical to the operation of your business that it cannot continue in the event of your illness or death, you should consider "key man" insurance. This type of policy is frequently required by banks or government loan programs. It also can be used to provide continuity in operations during a period of ownership transition caused by the death or incapacitation of an owner or other "key" employee.

- Automobile -- It is obvious that a vehicle owned by your business should be insured for both liability and replacement purposes. What is less obvious is that you may need special insurance (called "non-owned automobile coverage") if you use your personal vehicle on company business. This policy covers the business' liability for any damage which may result for such usage.

- Office and Director -- Under some circumstances, officers and directors of a corporation may become personally liable for their actions on behalf of the company. This type of policy covers this liability.

- Home Office -- If you are establishing an office in your home, it is a good idea to contact your homeowners' insurance company to update your policy to include coverage for office equipment. This coverage is not automatically included in a standard homeowner's policy.

FEDERAL AND STATE REGULATIONS

Sales Tax Number

In your state there is a percent sales and use tax which applies to the retail purchase, retail site, rental, storage, use or consumption of tangible personal property and certain services. In other words, sales tax must be collected on just about every tangible item sold.

A sales tax number is required for each business before opening. The number, plus instructions for collection, reporting and remitting the money to the state on a monthly basis, can be obtained by completing and submitting a Business Tax Registration Application to the state Department of Revenue. This license enables you to purchase tax-free and at wholesale rates.

Protection of Employees

All businesses with employees are required to comply with state and federal regulations regarding the protection of employees. For information on state labor laws, work force availability, prevailing wages, unemployment insurance, unionization, benefits packages and employment services contact your state government.

Federal information may be obtained by contacting the U.S. Department of Labor.

Unemployment Insurance Tax

Businesses are required by the state to pay unemployment insurance tax if the company has one or more employees for 20 weeks in a calendar year, or it has paid gross wages of $1,500 or more in a calendar year. The taxes are payable at a rate of 2.7 percent on the first $8,500 in annual wages of an employee. Go to your state home page to check the figures for your state.

Unemployment insurance must be reported and returns made to the state.

State Unemployment Tax (SUTA)

Immigration Act

The Federal Immigration Reform and Control Act of 1986 requires all employers to verify the employment eligibility of new employees. The law obligates an employer to have an Employment Eligibility Verification Form I-9 complete and on file for each employee. The Immigration and Naturalization Service Office of Business Liaison offers a selection of information bulletins and live assistance for this process through the Employer Hotline. In addition, INS forms and the Employer Handbook can be obtained by calling the Forms Hotline.

For Forms   1.800.870.3676
Employer Hotline   1.800.357.2099

FEDERAL AND STATE REGULATIONS ●●●●●●●

Occupational Safety and Health

The Federal Occupational Safety and Health Administration (OSHA) outlines specific health and safety standards employers must provide for the protection of employees. OSHA requires that if you employ more than 10 people, you maintain a record of on the job injuries on OSHA Form 200, which must be available for inspection and retained for five years. Many states have similar standards. For state information contact your local OSHA office.

OSHA - Department of Labor

Americans with Disabilities Act

This act of congress prohibits discrimination against people with disabilities and also requires employers to provide reasonable accommodations for such employees. Effective January 25, 1992, this act applies to companies with 25 or more employees. For more information about compliance with this law, contact:

US Architectural and Transportation Barriers Compliance Board
1.800.872.2253

Workman's Compensation

If a business employs three or more people, workers' compensation insurance must be carried to provide protection to those injured in on-the-job accidents. The State Board of Workers' Compensation aids people who need claim assistance or call your local insurance agent.

Minimum Wage

Virtually all business entities are subject to the federal minimum wage, overtime and child labor laws. Information on covered employees, child labor, training, wages, tipped employees, polygraph testing, substance abuse, hiring & firing, or other federal laws, may be obtained from:

U.S. Department of Labor
State Department of Labor, Licensing and Regulation

Alcohol Beverage Service

If you will be serving or selling alcoholic beverages, contact these agencies:

Federal Bureau of Alcohol, Tobacco and Firearms, US Department of Treasury
State Department of Revenue, Alcoholic Beverage Licensing

Day Care Licensing

Anyone conducting business involving groups of seniors or children must contact the state's Department of Social Services

Food or Cosmetic Related Business

If your business is involved with the production or packaging of food or cosmetics, contact:

Department of Agriculture

Manufacturing Related Information

If your business is related to manufacturing a product you need a manufacturer's registration number. To obtain a registration number (or textile products identification tag, if the product is pillows, blankets, mattresses, etc.), contact:

Federal Trade Commission
Consumer Response Center
Georgia
1.877.382.4357

Imports and Exports

If your business engages in importing and/or exporting, you can obtain special assistance from the US Department of Commerce

State Occupational & Professional Licensing Boards

Contact your state's occupational and professional licensing boards to obtain information above licensing procedures for these professional fields:

- Athletics
- Accountancy
- Amusement Rides
- Architectural Examiners
- Auctioneers
- Audiologists
- Barber Examiners
- Chiropractor Examiners
- Construction Contractors
- Cosmetology
- Engineers & Land Surveyors
- Environmental Certification Board
- Foresters
- Funeral Service

- Geologists
- Long Term Health Care
- Medical Examiners
- Motor Vehicle Management
- Nursing
- Occupational Therapy
- Opticianry
- Optometry
- Pharmacy
- Physical Therapy
- Pilotage (Port)
- Podiatry
- Pyrotechnic Safety Board
- Residential Builders Commission

Source: SBA.gov, "The U.S. Small Business Resource Guide"

BUSINESS ASSISTANCE PROGRAMS ●●●●●●

Small Business Administration (SBA)
The SBA's mission is to maintain and strengthen the nation's economy by aiding, counseling, assisting and protecting the interests of small businesses and by helping families and businesses recover from national disasters.

www.sba.gov

Service Corps of Retired Executives (SCORE)
SCORE is a SBA sponsored, national volunteer organization of retired executives, professionals, and business owners. They offer their time and expertise through no-fee confidential, one-on-one counseling, mentoring, and workshops.

www.score.org

Chamber of Commerce
The Chamber of Commerce is the unified voice of business and industry and the driving force to support its members' ability to be globally competitive and create jobs by maintaining a favorable legislative/regulatory balance with government, fostering a favorable climate with our members and their employees, and ensuring a quality work force, and encouraging environmental stewardship.

Local Chamber of Commerce
The Chamber gives your company access to networking, training, exposure, access to the membership in the Chamber.

State's Department of Commerce
The Department of Commerce is a state's lead agency for the growth and development of business and industry.

Local Library
Your local library may create, identify, and provide access to services, training, professional development, and information resources in support of small businesses and nonprofit organizations.

Minority Business Development Center (MBDC)
The MBDC is part of a national network that was established to increase the growth of new minority owned business and strengthen existing ones, therefore making them more profitable and creating new jobs. MBDC professional consultants offer a wide range of services that include initial counseling, government/private sector contracting assistance, financial management and more complex issues such as international trade franchising.

US Department of Commerce Minority Business Development Agency (MBDA)
Regional Office
401 W. Peachtree Street NW, Suite 1715
Atlanta, GA 30308

District Office
51 West First Avenue
Room 1314, Box 25
Miami, FL 33130

www.mbda.gov

MinorityAmerica.com
An internet source for companies and government agencies to find and buy from certified minority businesses

1401 Peachtree Street, Suite M102
Atlanta, GA 30309
Toll Free 877.517.7412

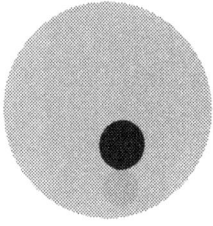

APPENDIX B:

GLOSSARY

GLOSSARY OF BUSINESS TERMS

Accounting
The recording, classifying, summarizing and interpreting in a significant manner and in terms of money, transactions and events of a financial character.

Accounts payable, AP
Bills to be paid as part of the normal course of business. This is a standard accounting term, one of the most common liabilities, which normally appears in the Balance Sheet listing of liabilities. Businesses receive goods or services from a vendor, receive an invoice, and until that invoice is paid the amount is recorded as part of "Accounts Payable."

Accounts receivable, AR
Debts owed to your company, usually from sales on credit. Accounts receivable is business asset, the sum of the money owed to you by customers who haven't paid. The standard procedure in business-to-business sales is that when goods or services are delivered the come with an invoice, which is to be paid later. Business customers expect to be invoiced and to pay later. The money involved goes onto the seller's books as accounts receivable, and onto the buyer's books as accounts payable.

Accumulated depreciation
Total accumulated depreciation reduces the formal accounting value (called book value) of assets. Each month's accumulated balance is the same as last month's balance plus this month's depreciation. Business Plan Pro shows accumulated depreciation in the Balance Sheet.

Acid test
Short-term assets minus accounts receivable and inventory, divided by short-term liabilities. This is a test of a company's ability to meet its immediate cash requirements. It is one of the more common business ratios used by financial analysts.

Acquisition costs
The incremental costs involved in obtaining a new customer.

Adaptive firm
An organization that is able to respond to and address changes in their market, their environment, and/or their industry to better position themselves for survival and profitability.

Advertising opportunity
A product or service may generate additional revenue through advertising if there is benefit from creating additional awareness, communicating differentiating attributes, hidden qualities or benefits. Optimizing the opportunity may involve leveraging strong emotional buying motives and potential benefits.

Agent
A business entity that negotiates, purchases, and/or sells, but does not take title to the goods.

Anchor tenant
Major store or supermarket that attracts customers to a shopping center.

Asset turnover
Sales divided by total assets. Important for comparison over time and to other companies of the same industry. This is a standard business ratio.

Assets

Property that a business owns, including cash and receivables, inventory, etc. Assets are any possessions that have value in an exchange. The more formal definition is the entire property of a person, association, corporation, or estate applicable or subject to the payment of debts. What most people understand as business assets are cash and investments, accounts receivable, inventory, office equipment, plant and equipment, etc. Assets can be long-term or short-term, and the distinction between these two categories might be whether they last three years, five years, 10 years, or whatever; normally the accountants decide for each company and what's important is consistency. The government also has a say in defining assets, because it has to do with tax treatment; when you buy a piece of equipment, if you call that purchase an expense then you can deduct it from taxable income. If you call it an asset you can't deduct it, but you can list it on your financial statement among the assets. The tax code controls how businesses decide to categorize spending into assets or expenses.

Assign lease

Tenant turns lease over to another business, which assumes payments and obligations under the lease.

Assumptions

The act of assuming/undertaking another's debts or obligations.

Auction

A public sale of goods to the highest bidder.

Automatic data processing

1. Data processing largely performed by automatic means.
2. The discipline which deals with methods and techniques of automatic data processing.
3. Pertaining to data processing equipment such as electrical accounting machines and electronic data processing equipment.

Bankruptcy

A condition in which a business cannot meet its debt obligations and petitions a federal district court for either reorganization of its debts or liquidation of its assets. In the action the property of a debtor is taken over by a receiver or trustee in bankruptcy for the benefit of the creditors. This action is conducted as prescribed by the National Bankruptcy Act, and may be voluntary or involuntary.

Benchmark

A benchmark is a standard or guideline used to compare some aspect of a business to some objective or external standard measure. For example, when a banker compares a business' profitability to standard financial ratios for that type of business, the process is sometimes referred to as "benchmarking." Business Plan Pro creates a chart that it calls "Business Benchmarks," which it uses to compare five standard business measures (sales, gross margin, net profits, collection days, and inventory turnover) as they change over time. In this case the benchmark is the business itself, so it compares past results to planned future results.

GLOSSARY OF BUSINESS TERMS ●●●●●●●

Business Information Center (BIC)
One of more than 50 specialized Small Business Administration units which offer the latest in high-technology hard-ware, software and telecommunications to assist small business PLUS one-on-one counseling with seasoned business veterans through the Service Corps of Retired Executives (SCORE). Each BIC offers electronic bulletin boards, computer data bases, on-line information exchange, periodicals and brochures, counseling, video tapes, reference materials, texts, start-up guides, application software, computer tutorials and interactive media.

Brand
A name, term, sign, symbol, design, or a combination of all used to uniquely identify a producer's goods and services and differentiate them from competitors.

Brand equity
The added value a brand name identity brings to a product or service beyond the functional benefits provided.

Brand extension strategy
The practice of using a current brand name to enter a new or different product class.

Brand recognition
Positions customer's relative perceptions of one brand to other competitive alternatives.

Break-even analysis
A technique commonly used to assess expected profitability of a company or a single product. The process determines at what point revenues equal expenditures based on fixed and variable. Breakeven is usually expressed in terms of the number of units sold or in total revenue. The break-even analysis is a standard financial analysis that measures general risk for a company by showing the sales level needed to cover both fixed and variable costs. That level of sales is called the break-even point, which can be stated as either unit sales volume or sales as dollar (or other currency) sales. The break-even analysis uses three assumptions to determine a break-even point: fixed costs, variable costs, and unit price. Fixed costs and variable costs are both included in this glossary, and unit price is the average revenue per unit of sales. The formula for break-even point in sales amount is:
$$= \text{fixed costs}/[1-(\text{Unit Variable Cost}/\text{Unit Price})]$$

The break-even analysis is often confused with payback period (see below), because many people interpret breaking even as paying back the initial investment. However, this is not what the break-even analysis actually does. Despite the common and more general use of the term "break even," the financial analysis has an exact definition as explained above. One important disadvantage of the break-even analysis is that it requires estimating a single per-unit variable cost, and a single per-unit price or revenue, for the entire business. That is a hard concept to estimate in a normal business that has a collection of products or services to sell. Another problem that comes up with break-even is its preference for talking about sales and variable cost of sales in units. Many businesses, especially service businesses, don't think of sales in unit, but rather as sales in money. In those cases, the break-even analysis should think of the dollar as the unit, and state variable costs per unit as variable costs per dollar of sales.

Break-even point

The break-even point in any business is that point at which the volume of sales or revenues exactly equals total expenses -- the point at which there is neither a profit nor loss -- under varying levels of activity. The break-even point tells the manager what level of output or activity is required before the firm can make a profit; reflects the relationship between costs, volume and profits.

The formula for break-even point in units is:
=Regular running costs/(Unit Price – Unit Variable Cost)

The formula for break-even point in sales amount is:
=Regular running costs/[1-(Unit Variable Cost/Unit Price)]

This should not be confused with the recovering initial investment through the regular operation of a business. That concept, often confused with break-even, is called the payback period.

Broker

An intermediary that serves as a go-between for the buyer or seller.

Bundling

The practice of marketing two or more product or service items in a single package with one price.

Burden rate

Refers to personnel burden, the sum of employer costs over and above salaries (including employer taxes, benefits, etc.). Business Plan Pro uses an assumed burden rate to calculate these extra personnel costs. The rate assumption is in the general assumptions table, as a percentage. Business Plan Pro applies this percentage to the straight wages and salaries. For example, if wages and salaries amount to $10,000 and the burden rate is 15%, then the personnel burden is $1,500, which is 15% of $10,000. The personnel burden is an operating expense, so it belongs with other expenses in the Profit and Loss table. It is also a personnel cost, so it also shows in the Personnel Plan table.

Business birth

The formation of a new establishment or enterprise.

Business death

The voluntary or involuntary closure of a firm or establishment.

Business dissolution

For enumeration purposes, the absence from any current record of a business that was present in a prior time period.

Business failure

The closure of a business causing a loss to at least one creditor.

Business mission

A brief description of an organization's purpose with reference to its customers, products or services, markets, philosophy, and technology.

GLOSSARY OF BUSINESS TERMS

Business plan
The written document that details a proposed or existing venture. It seeks to capture the vision, current status, expected needs, defined markets, and projected results of the business. A business plan "tells the entrepreneur's story" by describing the purpose, basis, reason and future of the venture.

Business start
For enumeration purposes, a business with a name or similar designation that did not exist in a prior time period.

Buy-sell agreement
An agreement designed to address situations in which one or more of the entrepreneurs wants to sell their interest in the venture.

C Corporation (C Corp)
Corporations are either the standard C corporation or the small business S corporation. The C corporation is the classic legal entity of the vast majority of successful companies in the United States. Most lawyers would agree that the C corporation is the structure that provides the best shielding from personal liability for owners, and provides the best non-tax benefits to owners. This is a separate legal entity, different from its owners, which pays its own taxes. Most lawyers would also probably agree that for a company that has ambitions of raising major investment capital and eventually going public, the C corporation is the standard form of legal entity. The S corporation is used for family companies and smaller ownership groups. The clearest distinction from C is that the S corporation's profits or losses go straight through to the S corporation's owners, without being taxed separately first. In practical terms, this means that the owners of the corporation can take their profits home without first paying the corporation's separate tax on profits, so those profits are taxed once for the S owner, and twice for the C owner. In practical terms the C corporation doesn't send its profits home to its owners as much as the S corporation does, because it usually has different goals and objectives. It often wants to grow and go public, or it already is public. In most states an S corporation is owned by a limited number (25 is a common maximum) of private owners, and corporations can't hold stock in S corporations, just individuals. Corporations can switch from C to S and back again, but not often. The IRS has strict rules for when and how those switches are made. You'll almost always want to have your CPA and in some cases your attorney guides you through the legal requirements for switching.

CAGR
Compound average growth rate. The standard formula is:
(last number/first number)^(1/periods)-1

CAM
Common area maintenance charges including property taxes, security, parking lot lighting and maintenance; may not apply to anchor tenants in retail leases.

Canceled loan
The annulment or recession of an approved loan prior to disbursement.

Cannibalization
The undesirable tradeoff where sales of a new product or service decrease sales from existing products or services and minimize or detract from the total revenue contribution of the organization.

Capital

1. Assets less liabilities, representing the ownership interest in a business;
2. A stock of accumulated goods, especially at a specified time and in contrast to income received during a specified time period;
3. Accumulated goods devoted to the production of goods; (4) accumulated possessions calculated to bring income.

Capital assets

Long-term assets, also known as Plant and Equipment, or fixed assets. These terms are interchangeable. Assets are generally divided into short-term and long-term assets, the distinction depending on how long they last. Usually the difference between short term and long term is a matter of accounting and financial policy. Five years is probably the most frequent division point, meaning that assets that depreciate over more than five years are long-term assets. Ten years and three years are also common. Business Plan Pro sets a starting value for capital assets in either the Start-up or the Past Performance table, depending of course on the nature of the company, whether it is start-up or ongoing. In the start-up table, the capital assets are called "." In the Past Performance table, they are labeled "Capital Assets." As the plan unfolds into months and year, depreciation decreases the net value of capital assets, and capital expenditure increases total assets. Depreciation appears in the Profit and Loss table, because it is an expense. Capital expenditure appears in the Cash Flow table, because it isn't an expense. Amounts typed into the Capital Expenditure row of the cash flow will increase the Capital Assets total in the Balance Sheet Table.

Capital expenditure

Spending on capital assets (also called plant and equipment, or fixed assets, or long-term assets). Capital expenditures are tracked in the Cash Flow table, because purchasing or selling assets affects cash flow, and the Balance Sheet table, but doesn't affect profit or loss. A positive amount typed into the Capital Expenditure row in the Cash Flow table will result in an increase in Capital Assets in the Balance Sheet, and a negative amount will result in a decrease in Capital Assets.

Capital input

This could also be called investment, or new investment. It is new money being invested in the business, not as loans or repayment of loans, but as money invested in ownership. This is also money at risk. It will grow in value if the business prospers, and decline in value if the business declines. This is closely related to the concept of paid-in capital, on the Balance Sheet table. Paid-in capital is the amount of money actually invested in the business as money, checks written by investors. Paid-in capital increases only when there is new investment. It is different from retained earnings. Business Plan Pro sets the initial amount of Paid-in Capital as an input into either the Start-up table (for start-up companies) or the Past Performance table (for ongoing companies.) After either of those initial entries, only New Investment Received (called "capital input" in earlier versions), in the Cash Flow table, increases Paid-in Capital. An entry as New Investment Received will increase your cash, and will also increase the total amount of paid-in capital. The amounts planned should be typed into the New Investment Received row of the Cash Flow table, and they will automatically increase Paid-in Capital in the Balance Sheet table.

Capitalized property

Personal property of the agency which has an average dollar value of $300.00 or more and a life expectancy of one year or more. Capitalized property shall be depreciated annually over the expected useful life to the agency.

GLOSSARY OF BUSINESS TERMS

Cash
Cash normally means bills and coins, as in paying in cash. However, the term is used in a business plan to represent the bank balance, or checking account balance. Business Plan Pro builds its financial analysis around cash and cash flow used in this second sense, as the balance of the checking account in the bank, plus other liquid securities used to bolster the checking account.

Cash discount
An incentive offered by the seller to encourage the buyer to pay within a stipulated time. For example, if the terms are 2/10/N 30, the buyer may deduct 2 percent from the amount of the invoice (if paid within 10 days) otherwise, the full amount is due in 30 days.

Cash flow
The cash flow in a business plan is the change in the cash balance. For example, the cash flow for a month would be a positive $10,000 if the balance was $10,000 at the beginning of the month and $20,000 at the end of the month. It is important to distinguish cash flow, which is the change in the balance, from cash or cash balance, which is the resulting ending balance. It is the amount of cash generated by the business after both expenses (including interest) and principal repayment on financing are paid More formally, cash flow is an assessment and understanding of cash coming into and flowing out of the venture in specific periods of time. This can be based on projections or actual cash flow and usually done on a monthly basis.

Cash flow budget
A budget that provides an overview of cash inflows and outflows during a specified period of time. This is often called the cash flow, or the cash budget. Just as cash flow is one of the most critical elements of business, the cash flow projection or table is one of the most critical elements of a business plan.

Central driving forces model
An entrepreneurial based model that considers the positives and negatives of three areas of the venture; founder(s), opportunities, and resources. The model then evaluates these areas regarding the "fits and gaps" that indicate correlating strengths or weaknesses for the venture. The CDF model also considers industry and market information in the overall analysis.

Channel conflicts
A situation where one or more channel members believe another channel member is engaged in behavior that is preventing it from achieving its goals. Channel conflict most often relates to pricing issues.

Channels of distribution
The system where customers are provided access to an organization's products or services.

Character
A letter, digit, or other symbol, that is a part of the organization, control, or representation of data used in computer systems.

Charge-Off
An accounting transaction removing an uncollectible balance from the active receivable accounts.

Charged Off Loan

An uncollectible loan for which the principal and accrued interest were removed from the receivable accounts.

Closing

Actions and procedures required to effect the documentation and disbursement of loan funds after the application has been approved, and the execution of all required documentation and its filing and recordation where required.

Closed Loan

Any loan for which funds have been disbursed, and all required documentation has been executed, received and reviewed. For statistical purposes, first or total disbursement is counted as a closed loan.

Co-branding

The pairing of two manufacture's brand names on a single product or service.

COGS

COGS, also written as cogs, is a shortcut for cost of goods sold. The cost of goods sold is traditionally the costs of materials and production of the goods a business sells. For a manufacturing company this is materials, labor, and factory overhead. For a retail shop it would be what it pays to buy the goods that it sells to its customers. For service businesses, that don't sell goods, the same concept is normally called "cost of sales," which shouldn't be confused with "sales and marketing expenses." The cost of sales in this case is directly analogous to cost of goods sold. For a consulting company, for example, the cost of sales would be the compensation paid to the consultants plus costs of research, photocopying, and production of reports and presentations. In standard accounting, costs of sales or costs of goods sold are subtracted from sales to calculate gross margin. These costs are distinguished from operating expenses, because gross profit is gross margin less operating expenses. Costs are not expenses.

Collateral

Something of value -- securities, evidence of deposit or other property -- pledged to support the repayment of an obligation.

Collateral document

A legal document covering the item(s) pledged as collateral on a loan, i.e., note, mortgages, assignment, etc.

Collection days

Collection days is supposed to represent the average number of days business waits, on average, between delivering an invoice and receiving payment. The formula for calculating collection days is:
=(Accounts receivable balance*360)/(Sales on credit*12) See Collection period, below.

Collection period (days)

The average number of days that pass between delivering an invoice and receiving the money. The formula is:
=(Accounts receivable balance*360)/(Sales on credit*12)

GLOSSARY OF BUSINESS TERMS

Commission
In business, a commission is the compensation paid to the person or entity based on the sale of a product; commonly calculated on a percentage basis. The most frequent commission formula is gross margin multiplied by the commission's percentage. To handle commissions with Business Plan Pro, use the spreadsheet programming capabilities to make one row of operating expenses depend on sales, or gross margin.

Commission's percent
An assumed percentage used to calculate commissions expense as the product of commission percent multiplied by sales, gross margin, or related sales items.

Competitive advantage
The strategic development where customers will choose a firm's product or service over its competitors based on significantly more favorable perceptions or offerings.

Competitive analysis
Assessing and analyzing the comparative strengths and weaknesses of competitors; may include their current and potential product and service development and marketing strategies.

Competitive entry wedges
Strategic competitive advantages and justification for entering an established market or activity that provides recognizable and known value. The four competitive entry wedges include: 1) New product or service 2) Parallel Competition 3) Franchise Entry 4) Twists

Compromise
The settlement of a claim resulting from a defaulted loan for less than the full amount due. Compromise settlement is a procedure available for use only in instances where the government cannot collect the full amount due within a reasonable time, by enforced collection proceedings or where the cost of such proceedings would not justify such effort.

Concentrated target marketing
A process that occurs when a single target market segment is pursued.

Consortium
A coalition of organizations, such as banks and corporations, set up to fund ventures requiring large capital resources.

Contingent Liability
A potential obligation that may be incurred dependent upon the occurrence of a future event. Two examples are: (1) the liability of an endorser or guarantor of a note if the primary borrower fails to pay as agreed and (2) the liability that would be incurred if a pending lawsuit is resolved in the other party's favor.

Contribution

Contribution can have different meanings in different context. When contribution is applied to a product or product line, it means the difference between total sales revenue and total variable costs, or, on a per-unit basis, the difference between unit selling and the unit variable cost and may be expressed in percentage terms (contribution margin) or dollar terms (contribution per unit). Contribution is also frequently expressed as contribution margin for a whole company or across a group or product line, in which case it can be taken as gross margin less sales and marketing expenses.

Contribution margin

Contribution can have different meanings in different context. When contribution is applied to a product or product line, it means the difference between total sales revenue and total variable costs, or, on a per-unit basis, the difference between unit selling and the unit variable cost and may be expressed in percentage terms (contribution margin) or dollar terms (contribution per unit). Contribution is also frequently expressed as contribution margin for a whole company or across a group or product line, in which case it can be taken as gross margin less sales and marketing expenses. For example, Marketing Plan Pro produces a table named Contribution Margin that shows sales, cost of sales, gross margin, sales and marketing expenses, and contribution margin. The contribution is gross margin less sales and marketing expenses.

Core marketing strategy

A statement that communicates the predominant reason to buy to a specific target market.

Corporation

Corporations are either the standard C corporation or the small business S corporation. The C corporation is the classic legal entity of the vast majority of successful companies in the United States. Most lawyers would agree that the C corporation is the structure that provides the best shielding from personal liability for owners, and provides the best non-tax benefits to owners. This is a separate legal entity, different from its owners, which pays its own taxes. Most lawyers would also probably agree that for a company that has ambitions of raising major investment capital and eventually going public, the C corporation is the standard form of legal entity. The S corporation is used for family companies and smaller ownership groups. The clearest distinction from C is that the S corporation's profits or losses go straight through to the S corporation's owners, without being taxed separately first. In practical terms, this means that the owners of the corporation can take their profits home without first paying the corporation's separate tax on profits, so those profits are taxed once for the S owner, and twice for the C owner. In practical terms the C corporation doesn't send its profits home to its owners as much as the S corporation does, because it usually has different goals and objectives. It often wants to grow and go public, or it already is public. In most states an S corporation is owned by a limited number (25 is a common maximum) of private owners, and corporations can't hold stock in S corporations, just individuals. Corporations can switch from C to S and back again, but not often. The IRS has strict rules for when and how those switches are made. You'll almost always want to have your CPA and in some cases your attorney guide you through the legal requirements for switching. The process of incorporating should be completed with the state's secretary of state or state corporate counsel.

Corridor principal

The principal where an entrepreneurial venture may find that it has significantly changed its focus from the initial concept of the venture as it has continually responded and adapted to its market and the desire to optimize profitability potential.

Costs

Money obligated for goods and services received during a given period of time, regardless of when ordered or whether paid for.

Cost of goods sold

The cost of goods sold is traditionally the costs of materials and production of the goods a business sells. For a manufacturing company this is materials, labor, and factory overhead. For a retail shop it would be what it pays to buy the goods that it sells to its customers. For service businesses, that don't sell goods, the same concept is normally called "cost of sales," which shouldn't be confused with "sales and marketing expenses." The cost of sales in this case is directly analogous to cost of goods sold. For a consulting company, for example, the cost of sales would be the compensation paid to the consultants plus costs of research, photocopying, and production of reports and presentations. In standard accounting, costs of sales or costs of goods sold are subtracted from sales to calculate gross margin. These costs are distinguished from operating expenses, because gross profit is gross margin less operating expenses. Costs are not expenses.

Cost of sales

The costs associated with producing the sales. In a standard manufacturing or distribution company, this is about the same as the cost of the goods sold. In a services company, this is more likely to be personnel costs for people delivering the service, or subcontracting costs. This term is commonly used interchangeably with "cost of goods sold," particularly when it is for a manufacturing, retail, distribution, or other product-based company. In these cases it is traditionally the costs of materials and production of the goods a business sells. For a manufacturing company this is materials, labor, and factory overhead. For a retail shop it would be what it pays to buy the goods that it sells to its customers. For service businesses, that don't sell goods, the same concept is normally called "cost of sales," which shouldn't be confused with "sales and marketing expenses." The cost of sales in this case is directly analogous to cost of goods sold. For a consulting company, for example, the cost of sales would be the compensation paid to the consultants plus costs of research, photocopying, and production of reports and presentations. In standard accounting, costs of sales or costs of goods sold are subtracted from sales to calculate gross margin. These costs are distinguished from operating expenses, because gross profit is gross margin less operating expenses. Costs are not expenses. For example the Sales Forecast in and Marketing Plan Pro for a simple consulting company includes cost of sales as an estimate of the cost of fulfilling consulting.

Credit rating

A grade assigned to a business concern to denote the net worth and credit standing to which the concern is entitled in the opinion of the rating agency as a result of its investigation.

Cross elasticity of demand

The change in the quantity demanded of one product or service impacting the change in demand for another product or service.

Current assets

The same as short-term assets.

Current debt

Short-term debt, short-term liabilities.

Current liabilities
Short-term debt, short-term liabilities.

Data element
The basic unit of identifiable and definable information. A data element occupies the space provided by fields in a record or blocks on a form. It has an identifying name and value or values for expressing a specific fact. For example, a data element named "Color of Eyes" could have recorded values of "Blue (a name)," "Bl (an abbreviation)," "06 (a code)." Similarly, a data element named "Age of Employee" could have a recorded value of "28" (a numeric value).

DBA (doing business as)
DBA stands for "Doing Business As," which is a company name, also commonly called a "Fictitious business name." When a sole proprietor operates a company using any name except his or her own given name, then the DBA or fictitious business name registration establishes the legal ownership to satisfy banks, local authorities, and customers. So when you start the Acme Restaurant, unless you are named Acme, you need your DBA to open a bank account in that name, pay employees, and do business. You can usually obtain this registration through the county government, and the cost is no more than a small registration fee plus a required newspaper ad, for a total of less than $100 in most states.

Debenture
Debt instrument evidencing the holder's right to receive interest and principal installments from the named obligor. Applies to all forms of unsecured, long-term debt evidenced by a certificate of debt.

Debt capital
Business financing that normally requires periodic interest payments and repayment of the principal within a specified time.

Debt and equity
The sum of liabilities and capital. This should always be equal to total assets.

Debt financing
The provision of long term loans to small business concerns in exchange for debt securities or a note.

Deed of trust
A document under seal which, when delivered, transfers a present interest in property. May be held as collateral.

Defaults
The nonpayment of principal and/or interest on the due date as provided by the terms and conditions of the note.

Deferred Loan
Loans whose principal and or interest installments are postponed for a specified period of time.

Depreciation
An accounting and tax concept used to estimate the loss of value of assets over time. For example, cars depreciate with use.

Differentiated target marketing
A process that occurs when an organization simultaneously pursues several different market segments, usually with a different strategy for each.

Differentiation
An approach to create a competitive advantage based on obtaining a significant value difference that customers will appreciate and be willing to pay for, and which ideally will increase their loyalty as a result.

Direct mail marketing
A form of direct marketing that involves sending information through a mail process, physical or electronic, to potential customers.

Direct marketing
Any method of distribution that gives the customer access to an organization's products and services without intermediaries; also, any communication from the producer that communicates with a target market to generate a revenue producing response.

Directory
A computer term related to the operating system on IBM and compatible computers. Disk storage space is divided into directories.

Disbursement
The actual payout to borrower of loan funds, in whole or part. It may be concurrent with the closing, or follow it.

Disbursing officer
An employee authorized to pay out cash or issue checks in settlement of vouchers approved by a certifying officer.

Distinctive competency
An organization's strengths or qualities including skills, technologies, or resources that distinguish it from competitors to provide superior and unique customer value and, hopefully, is difficult to imitate.

Diversification
A product-market strategy that involves the development or acquisition of offerings new to the organization and/or the introduction of those offerings to the target markets not previously served by the organization.

Divestiture
Change of ownership and/or control of a business from a majority (non-disadvantaged) to disadvantaged persons.

Dividends
Money distributed to the owners of a business as profits.

Dual distribution
The practice of simultaneously distributing products or services through two or more marketing channels that may or may not compete for similar buyers.

Early adopters
One type of adopter in Everett Rogers' diffusion of innovations framework that describes buyers that follow "innovators" rather than be the first to purchase.

Early majority
One type of adopter in Everett Rogers' diffusion of innovations framework that describes those interested in new technology that wait to purchase until these innovations are proven to perform to the expected standard.

Earning Power
The demonstrated ability of a business to earn a profit, over time, while following good accounting practices. When a business shows a reasonable profit on invested capital after fully maintaining the business property, appropriately compensating its owner and employees, servicing its obligations, and fully recognizing its costs, the business may be said to have demonstrated earning power. Demonstrated earning power is the foremost test of the business risk in pressing upon an application for a loan.

Earnings
Also called income or profits, earnings are the famous "bottom line": sales less costs of sales and expenses.

Easement
A right or privilege that a person may have on another's land, as the right of a way or ingress or egress.

EBIT
Earnings before interest and taxes.

Economies of scale
The benefit that larger production volumes allow fixed costs to be spread over more units lowering the average unit costs and offering a competitive price and margin advantage. Producing in large volume often generates economies of scale. The per-unit cost of something goes down with volume because vendors charge less per unit for larger orders, and often production techniques and facilities cost less per unit as volume increases. Fixed costs are spread over larger volume.

Effective demand
When prospective buyers have the willingness and ability to purchase an organization's offerings.

Effective tax rate
The effective tax rate is a comparison of final tax payments compared to actual profits. Usually the effective tax rate is somewhat less than the nominal tax rate because of deductions, credits, etc.

EIH
Entrepreneur in Heat describes an entrepreneur that continues to develop new products and services beyond what the venture can support and inadvertently may diminish the focus and effectiveness of the activities supporting the venture's primary revenue streams.

Employee Assistance Program (EAP) Coordinator
Coordinates the activities of Central Office or regional counselors, maintains a community resource list, of available professional assistance to troubled employees and a current roster of EAP counselors for the area of his/her jurisdiction.

EAP Counselor
Conducts confidential consultations with troubled employees who so request or who are referred for objective analysis of a personal problem and for identification of the best available assistance and/or professional services needed to resolve the employee's problem.

Enterprise
Aggregation of all establishments owned by a parent company. An enterprise can consist of a single, independent establishment or it can include subsidiaries or other branch establishments under the same ownership and control.

Entrepreneur
One who assumes the financial risk of the initiation, operation and management of a given business or undertaking.

Equity
An ownership interest in a business; capital. Equity can be calculated as the difference between assets and liabilities.

Equity financing
The sales of some portion of ownership in a venture to gain additional capital for start-up without any guaranteed return, but with the opportunity to share in the company's profits. Equity financing includes long-term subordinated securities containing stock options and/or warrants.

Equity partnership
A limited partnership arrangement for providing start-up and seed capital to businesses.

Escrow accounts
Funds placed in trust with a third party, by a borrower for a specific purpose and to be delivered to the borrower only upon the fulfillment of certain conditions.

Establishment
A single-location business unit, which may be independent -- called a single- establishment enterprise-- or owned by a parent enterprise.

Evaluating ideas and opportunities
The process of considering ideas versus opportunities, and then screening those opportunities using objective criteria as well as personal criteria.

Everett Rogers
Author who studied and published work on the diffusion of innovation.

Exclusive distribution
A distribution strategy whereby a producer sells its products or services in only one retail outlet in a specific geographical area.

Exclusivity provision
Shopping center can't lease to another who provides the same product or service that existing tenant does.

Expense

Webster's calls it "a spending or consuming; disbursement, expenditure. What's important about expenses for the purpose of business accounting is that expenses are deductible against taxable income. Common expenses are rent, salaries, advertising, travel, etc. Questions arise because some businesses have trouble distinguishing between expenses and purchase of assets, especially with development expenses. When your business purchases office equipment, if you call that an expense then you can deduct that amount from taxable income, so it reduces taxes.

Experience curve

A visual representation, often based on a function of time, from exposure to a process that offers greater information and results in enhanced efficiency and operations advantage.

FAB

Features, Advantages, and Benefits Analysis

A FAB analysis explores the features, advantages, and benefits of a product or service offering. Marketing plans need to understand these concepts in order to develop effective marketing programs.

People often confuse features and benefits. For example, in an automobile, air bags are a feature that produce the benefit of greater safety. Advantages fall in between, features become advantages that offer benefits to the end user.

Failure rule, common causes

Entrepreneurial ventures most often fail due to one or more of these four issues: 1) Inadequate sales (39%) 2) Competitive weaknesses (21%) 3) Excessive operating expenses (11%) 4) Uncollected receivables (9%).

Failure rule, exceptions to the rule

Exceptions to the failure rule include: 1) High potential ventures 2) Threshold concept 3) Promise of growth 4) Venture Capital backing

Fatal 2% rule

The concept that if a venture can just get "2%" of total market share it will be successful. This percentage can be unattainable based on the approach, limited resources, and/or structure of the industry.

Fighting brand strategy

Adding a new brand to confront competitive brands in an established product category.

Financial reports

Reports commonly required from applicants request for financial assistance, e.g.:

1. Balance Sheet - A report of the status of a firm's assets, liabilities and owner's equity at a given time.
2. Income Statement - A report of revenue and expense which shows the results of business operations or net income for a specified period of time.
3. Cash Flow - A report which analyzes the actual or projected source and disposition of cash during a past or future accounting period.

Financing

New funds provided to a business, by either loans or purchase of debt securities or capital stock.

First mover advantage
Key first mover advantages include: 1) Reputation effect 2) Experience curve 3) Customer commitment and loyalty

First mover disadvantage
These factors can turn first-mover advantages into weaknesses. They include: 1) Resolution of technological uncertainty 2) Resolution of strategic uncertainty 3) Free-rider effect - others duplicate based on the leader's success 4) Complementary assets to exploit core technological expertise

Fiscal year
Standard accounting practice allows the accounting year to begin in any month. Fiscal years are numbered according to the year in which they end. For example, a fiscal year ending in February of 1992 is Fiscal 1992, even though most of the year takes place in 1991.

Five forces model
Porter's model that considers these forces as they impact and industry and the overall competitive climate: 1) Risk of entry by potential competitors 2) Bargaining power of suppliers 3) Bargaining power of buyers 4) Threat of substitute products 5) Rivalry among established firms

Fixed cost
Running costs that take time to wind down: usually rent, overhead, some salaries. Technically, fixed costs are those that the business would continue to pay even if it went bankrupt. In practice, fixed costs are usually considered the running costs. These are static expenses that do not fluctuate with output volume and become progressively smaller per unit of output as volume increases. Fixed costs are an important assumption for developing a break-even analysis. The standard break-even formula estimates a break-even point of sales based on per-unit price or revenue, per-unit variable costs, and fixed costs.

Flow chart
A graphical representation for the definition, analysis, or solution of a problem, in which symbols are used to represent operations, data, flow, equipment, etc.

Focus group
Small groups of people, usually between 9 and 12 in number, representing target audiences, that are brought together to discuss a topic that will offer insight for product development and/or marketing efforts.

Foreclosure
The act by the mortgagee or trustee upon default, in the payment of interest or principal of a mortgage of enforcing payment of the debt by selling the underlying security.

Forms of market research
Market research can be casual, affordable, and effective for the entrepreneur. Jay Conrad Levinson provides examples of this form of market research approach in "Guerrilla Marketing Attack."

GLOSSARY OF BUSINESS TERMS

Franchising
A continuing relationship in which the franchisor provides a licensed privilege to the franchisee to do business, and offers assistance in organizing, training, merchandising, marketing and managing in return for a consideration. Franchising is a form of business by which the owner (franchisor) of a product, service or method obtains distribution through affiliated dealers (franchisees). The product, method or service being marketed is usually identified by the franchisor's brand name, and the holder of the privilege (franchisee) is often given exclusive access to a defined geographical area.

Frequency marketing
Activities which encourage repeat purchasing through a formal program enrollment process to develop loyalty and commitment from the customer base. Frequency marketing is also referred to as loyalty programs.

Full-cost price strategies
Costs that consider variable and fixed cost (total cost) in the pricing of a product of service

Future value projections
The process of projecting the future value of a venture and/or an investment in the venture. It typically considers an expected rate of return, inflation, and the period of time to assess future value.

Goodwill
When a company purchases another company for more than the value of its assets -- which is quite common -- the difference is recorded as an asset named "Goodwill." This is not a general term for the value of a brand, for example, but a very specific accounting term. For example, if one business buys another business for $1 million then it needs to show the $1 million spent as an asset. If there are only $500 thousand in real assets, the accounting result should be $500,000 in real assets purchased and another $500,000 in "Goodwill."

Gross margin
The difference between total sales revenue and total cost of goods sold (also called total cost of sales). This can also be expressed on a per unit basis, as the difference between unit selling price and unit cost of goods sold. Gross margin can be expressed in dollar or percentage terms.

Gross margin percent
Gross margin divided by sales, displayed as a percentage. Acceptable levels depend on the nature of the business. There are providers who can deliver standard gross margins for different types of industries based on SIC (Standard Industry Classification) codes that categorize industries.

Gross Domestic Product (GDP)
The most comprehensive single measure of aggregate economic output. Represents the market value of the total output of the goods and services produced by a nation's economy.

Gross Lease
Tenant pays flat monthly amount; landlord pays all operating costs, including property taxes, insurance and utilities.

Gross National Product (GNP)

A measure of a nation's aggregate economic output. Since 1991 GDP, a slightly different calculation, has replaced GNP as a measure of U.S. economic output.

Guaranteed loan

A loan made and serviced by a lending institution under agreement that a governmental agency will purchase the guaranteed portion if the borrower defaults.

Guerilla marketing investment strategy

This is an inverse approach to traditional marketing budgeting. Levinson states: Invest 10% in the "universe" Invest 30% in you prospects Invest 60% in your customers

Guerrilla marketing

Examples of mini, maxi, and non-media tools: Mini: canvassing, personal letters, calls, circulars, brochures, classified ads, Maxi: yellow pages and signs Non-Media: public relations, advertising

Guerrilla marketing: concept

Effective and pragmatic marketing can be done with limited resources and should focus on meeting the needs of existing customers in everything that is done, while building the base of prospects through creating additional awareness within the market.

Hardware

A term used to describe the mechanical, electrical and electronic elements of a data processing system.

Harvesting

Harvesting is most often referring to selling a business or product line, as when a company sells a product line or division or a family sells a business. Harvesting is also occasionally used to refer to sales of a product or product line towards the end of a product life cycle.

Hazard Insurance

Insurance required showing lender as loss payee covering certain risks on real and personal property used for securing loans.

Ideas versus opportunities

Ideas are the basis of potential business opportunities. Good ideas do not necessarily represent good opportunities.

Income statement

Also called Profit and Loss statement. An income statement is a financial statement that shows sales, cost of sales, gross margin, operating expenses, and profits or losses. Gross margin is sales less cost of sales, and profit (or loss) is gross margin less operating expenses and taxes. The result is profit if it's positive, loss if it's negative.

Incubator

A facility designed to encourage entrepreneurship and minimize obstacles to new business formation and growth, particularly for high technology firms, by housing a number of fledgling enterprises that share an array of services. These shared services may include meeting areas, secretarial services, accounting services, research libraries, on-site financial and management counseling and word processing facilities.

Independent and Qualified Public Accountants

Public accountants are independent when neither they nor any of their family have a material, direct or indirect financial interest in the borrower other than as an accountant. They are qualified, unless there is contrary evidence, when they are either (1) certified, licensed, or otherwise registered if so required by the state in which they work, or (2) have worked as a public accountant for at least five years and are accepted by SBA.

Industrial Revenue Bond (IRB)

A tax-exempt bond issued by a state or local government agency to finance industrial or commercial projects that serve a public good. The bond usually is not backed by the full faith and credit of the government that issues it, but is repaid solely from the revenues of the project and requires a private sector commitment for repayment.

Initial Public Offering (IPO)

A corporation's initial efforts of raising capital through the sale of securities on the public stock market.

Innovation

Introduction of a new idea into the marketplace in the form of a new product or service, or an improvement in organization or process.

Innovation: Evolutionary or Revolutionary

The determination if an innovation is a "new and improved" concept taken to the next level (evolutionary), or the rare innovation that revolutionizes a technology or concept to the product or services.

Innovators

One type of adopter in Everett Rogers' diffusion of innovations framework describing the first group to purchase a new product or service.
INSOLVENCY   The inability of a borrower to meet financial obligations as they mature, or having insufficient assets to pay legal debts.

Integrated marketing communications

The practice of blending different elements of the communication mix in mutually reinforcing ways.

Intensive distribution

A distribution strategy whereby a producer attempts to sell its products or services in as many retail outlets as possible within a geographical area without exclusivity.

Interest

An amount paid a lender for the use of funds.

Interest expense

Interest is paid on debts, and interest expense is deducted from profits as expenses. Interest expense is either long-term or short-term interest.

Intrapreneurship

Entrepreneurial-based activities within a corporation that receive organizational support and resources commitments for the purpose of an innovative new business experience within the organization itself.

Inventory
Goods in stock, either finished goods or materials to be used to manufacture goods.

Inventory turnover
Total cost of sales divided by inventory. Usually calculated using the average inventory over an accounting period, not an ending-inventory value.

Inventory turns
Inventory turnover (above). Total cost of sales divided by inventory. Usually calculated using the average inventory over an accounting period, not an ending-inventory value.

Inverse order of maturity
When payments are received from borrowers that are larger than the authorized repayment schedules the overpayment is credited to the final installments of the principal which reduces the maturity of the loan and does not affect the original repayment schedule.

Investment banking
Businesses specializing in the formation of capital. This is done by outright purchase and sale of securities offered by the issuer, standby underwriting or "best efforts selling."

Invitation for bids
Formal solicitations for offerings, to perform procurements by competitive bids when the specifications describe the requirements of the government clearly, accurately, and completely; but avoiding unnecessarily restrictive specifications or requirements which might unduly limit the number of bidders.

Jobber
An intermediary that buys from producers to sell to retailers and offers various services with that function.

Job description
A written statement listing the elements of a particular job or occupation, e.g., purpose, duties, equipment used, qualifications, training, physical and mental demands, working conditions, etc.

Judgment
Judicial determination of the existence of indebtedness, or other legal liability.

Judgment by confession
The act of debtors permitting judgment to be entered against them for a given sum with a statement to that effect, without the institution of legal proceedings.

Junk bond
A high-yield corporate bond issue with a below-investment rating that became a growing source of corporate funding in the 1980s.

Labor
The labor costs associated with making goods to be sold. This labor is part of the cost of sales, part of the manufacturing and assembly. The row heading refers to fulfillment costs as well, for service companies.

Laggards
One type of adopter in Everett Rogers' diffusion of innovations framework describing the risk adverse group that follows the late majority that is generally not interested in new technology and are the last group of customers to buy.

LBO
A type of purchase of a business that relies heavily on the venture's cash receipts with expectations of positive cash flow continuing based on historical or other performance indicators.

Lease
A contract between the owner (lessor) and the tenant (lessee) stating the conditions under which the tenant may occupy or use the property.

Legal Rate Of Interest
The maximum rate of interest fixed by the laws of the various states, which a lender may charge a borrower for the use of money.

Lending Institution
Any institution, including a commercial bank, savings and loan association, commercial finance company, or other lender qualified to participate with SBA in the making of loans.

Lessor
Landlord

Lessee
Tenant

Leveraged buy-out (LBO)
A type of purchase of a business that relies heavily on the venture's cash receipts with expectations of positive cash flow continuing based on historical or other performance indicators. Financing provided largely by borrowed money, often in the form of junk bonds.

Liabilities
Debts; money that must be paid. Usually debt on terms of less than five years is called short-term liabilities, and debt for longer than five years in long-term liabilities.

Lien
A charge upon or security interest in real or personal property maintained to ensure the satisfaction of a debt or duty ordinarily arising by operation of law.

Life cycle
A model depicting the sales volume cycle of a single product, brand, service or a class of products or services over time described in terms of the four phases of introduction, growth, maturity and decline.

Limited Liability Company (LLC)

The LLC form is different for different states, with some real advantages in some states that aren't relevant in others. An LLC is usually a lot like an S corporation, a combination of some limitation on legal liability and some favorable tax treatment for profits and transfer of assets. This is a newer form of legal entity, and often harder to establish than a corporation. Why would you establish an LLC instead of a corporation? That's a tough legal question, not one we can answer here. In general, the LLC has to be missing two of the four characteristics of a corporation (limited liability, centralized management, continuity of life, and free transferability of ownership interest). Still, with the advisability and advantages varying from state to state, here again, this is a question to take to a good local attorney with small business experience.

Liquidation

The disposal, at maximum prices, of the collateral securing a loan, and the voluntary and enforced collection of the remaining loan balance from the obligators and/or guarantors.

Liquidation value

The net value realizable in the sale (ordinarily a forced sale) of a business or a particular asset.

Litigation

[1]Refers to a loan in "liquidation status" which has been referred attorneys for legal action. [2]The practice of taking legal action through the judicial process.

LLC (Limited Liability Company)

The LLC form is different for different states, with some real advantages in some states that aren't relevant in others. An LLC is usually a lot like an S corporation, a combination of some limitation on legal liability and some favorable tax treatment for profits and transfer of assets. This is a newer form of legal entity, and often harder to establish than a corporation. Why would you establish an LLC instead of a corporation? That's a tough legal question, not one we can answer here. In general, the LLC has to be missing two of the four characteristics of a corporation (limited liability, centralized management, continuity of life, and free transferability of ownership interest). Still, with the advisability and advantages varying from state to state, here again, this is a question to take to a good local attorney with small business experience.

Loan agreement

Agreement to be executed by borrower, containing pertinent terms, conditions, covenants and restrictions.

Loan payoff amount

The total amount of money needed to meet a borrower's obligation on a loan. It is arrived at by accruing gross interest for one day and multiplying this figure by the number of days that exist between the date of the last repayment and the date on which the loan is to be completely paid off. This amount, known as accrued interest, is combined with the latest principal and escrow balances that are applicable to what is now referred to as the loan payoff amount. In the case where prepaid interest exceeds the accrued interest the latter is subtracted from the former and the difference is used to reduce the total amount owed.

Long term assets

Assets like plant and equipment that are depreciated over terms of more than five years, and are likely to last that long, too.

Long term interest rate

The interest rate charged on long-term debt.

Long term liabilities
This is the same as long-term loans. Most companies call a debt long-term when it is on terms of five years or more.

Loss
Loss is an accounting concept, the exact opposite of profit, normally the bottom line of the Income Statement, which is also called Profit or Loss statement. Start with sales, subtract all costs of sales and all expenses, and that produces profit before tax. Subtract tax to get net profit. If the end result is negative, then instead of profit it is called loss.

Loss rate
A rate developed by comparing the ratio of total loans charged off to the total loans disbursed from inception of the program to the present date.

Loss reserve adjustment rate
A reserve rate based upon the ratio of the aggregate net charge offs (charge offs less recoveries) for the most recent five years to the total average loans outstanding for the comparable 5-year period.

Loyalty programs
Activities designed to encourage repeat purchasing through a formal program enrollment process and the distribution of benefits. Loyalty programs may also be referred to as frequency marketing.

Manufacturer's Agent
An agent who typically operates on an extended contractual basis, often sells in an exclusive territory, offers non-competing but related lines of goods, and has defined authority regarding prices and terms of sale.

Market
Prospective buyers, individuals or organizations, willing and able to purchase the organization's potential offering.

Market development funds
The monetary resources a company invests to assist channel members increase volume sales of their products or services. Hereafter referred to by the acronym MDF.

Market evolution
Changes in primary demand for a product class and changes in technology.

Market Plan: Its purpose and components
Often found within the business plan, the market plan provides details regarding the overall marketing strategy, pricing, sales tactics, service and warranty policies, advertising and promotion and distribution plans for the venture.

Market redefinition
Changes in the offering demanded by buyers or promoted by competitors to enhance its perception and associated sales.

Market sales potential

The maximum level of sales that might be available to all organizations serving a defined market in a specific time period.

Market segmentation

The categorization of potential buyers into groups based on common characteristics such as age, gender, income, and geography or other attributes relating to purchase or consumption behavior.

Market share

Total sales of an organization divided by the sales of the market they serve.

Market-development strategy

A product-market strategy whereby an organization introduces its offerings to markets other than those it is currently serving. In global marketing, this strategy can be implemented through exportation licensing, join ventures or direct investment.

Market-penetration strategy

A product market strategy hereby an organization seeks to gain greater dominance in a market in which it already has an offering. This strategy often focuses on capturing a larger share of an existing market.

Marketing

The set of planned activities designed to positively influence the perceptions and purchase choices of individuals and organizations.

Marketing audit

A comprehensive and systematic examination of a company's or business unit's marketing environment, objectives, strategies, and activities with a view of identifying and understanding problem areas and opportunities, and recommending a plan of action.

Marketing mix

The activities controllable by the organization and include the product, service, or idea offered, the manner in which the offering will be communicated to customers, the method for distributing or delivering the offering, and the price to be charged for

Marketing plan

A written document containing description and guidelines for an organization's or a product's marketing strategies, tactics and programs for offering their products and services over the defined planning period, often one year.

Marketing-cost analysis

Assigning or allocating costs to a specified marketing activity or entity in a manner that accurately captures the financial contribution of activities or entities to the organization.

Markup

Markup is the difference between invoice cost and selling price. It may be expressed either as a percentage of the selling price or the cost price or is supposed to cover all the costs of doing business plus a profit. Whether markup is based on the selling price or the cost price, the base is always equal to 100 percent.

Materials
Included in the cost of sales. These are materials involved in the assembly or manufacture of goods for sale.

Maturity
As applied to securities and commercial paper, the period end date when payment of principal is due.

Maturity extensions
Extensions of payment beyond the original period established for repayment of a loan.

Mission statement
A statement that captures an organization's purpose, customer orientation and business philosophy.

Merger
A combination of two or more corporations wherein the dominant unit absorbs the passive ones, the former continuing operation usually under the same name. In a consolidation two units combine and are succeeded by a new corporation, usually with a new title.

Mortgage
An instrument giving legal title to secure the repayment of a loan made by the mortgagee (lender). In legal contemplation there are two types: (1) title theory - operates as a transfer of the legal title of the property to the mortgagee, and (2) lien theory - creates a lien upon the property in favor of the mortgagee.

Moving Weighted Average
Moving weighted average is a statistical method to forecast the future based on past results. It is a subset of time series analysis. Detailed explanation goes beyond the scope of a glossary of terms, but should be included in any text on forecasting, statistics, or business forecasting.
For an immediate explanation, go to your favorite Internet searcher and search for the term "moving weighted average."

Multiple-channel system
A channel of distribution that uses a combination of direct and indirect channels where the channel members serve different segments.

Negotiation
The "face to face" process used by local unions and the employer to exchange their views on those matters involving personnel policies and practices, or other matters affecting the working conditions of employees in the unit and reduced to a written binding agreement. Used also by contracting officers to reach agreement with potential contractors.

Negotiation dispute
That point in negotiations where labor and management cannot come to an agreement on some or all of the issues on the bargaining table and the services of the FMCS have not been utilized.

Negotiated grievance procedure
The sole and exclusive procedure available to all employees in a bargaining unit and the employer for processing grievances and disputes.

GLOSSARY OF BUSINESS TERMS

Net worth
Property owned (assets), minus debts and obligations owed (liabilities), is the owner's equity (net worth).

Net cash flow
This is the projected change in cash position, an increase or decrease in cash balance.

Net Present Value (NPV)
The method of discounting future streams of income using an expected rate of return to evaluate the current value of expected earnings. It calculates future value in today's dollars. NPV may be used to determine the current value of a business being offered for sale or capitalized.

Net profit
The operating income less taxes and interest. The same as earnings, or net income.

Net profit margin before taxes
The remainder after cost of goods sold, other variable costs revenue, or simply, total revenue minus total cost. Net profit margin can be expressed in actual monetary values or percentage terms.

New-brand strategy
The development of a new brand and often a new offering for a product class that has not been previously served by the organizations.

Non-disturbance Clause
Tenant cannot be forced to move or sign a new lease if building or shopping center is sold or undergoes foreclosure.

Not Invented Here (NIH)
A negative response to innovations and inventions from sources outside the venture's own research and development activities.

Notes and accounts receivable
A secured or unsecured receivable evidenced by a note or open account arising from activities involving liquidation and disposal of loan collateral.

Obligations
Technically defined as "amount of orders placed, contracts awarded, services received, and similar transactions during a given period which will require payments during the same or a future period."

Offering
The total benefits or satisfaction provided to target markets by an organization. An offering consists of a tangible product or service plus related services such as installation, repair, warranties or guarantees, packaging, technical support, field support, and other services.

Offering mix or portfolio
The complete array of an organization's offerings including all products and services.

Operating leverage
The extent to which fixed costs and variable costs are used in the production and marketing of products and services.

Operations control
The practice of assessing how well an organization performs marketing activities as it seeks to achieve planned outcomes.

Opportunity analysis
The process of identifying and exploring revenue enhancement or expense reduction situations to better position the organization to realize increased profitability, efficiencies, market potential or other desirable objectives.

Opportunity cost
Resource use options that are given up as a consequence of pursuing one activity among several possibilities. Potential benefits foregone as a result of choosing an alternative course of action.

Ordinary interest
Simple interest based on a year of 360 days, contrasting with exact interest having a base year of 365 days.

Original equipment manufacturer (OEM)
The process that is facilitated through licensing or other financial arrangements where the initial producer of a product or service enters into an agreement to allow another entity to include, remanufacture, or label products or services under their own name and sell through their distribution channels. It typically results in a "higher volume, lower margin" relationship for the original producer, and offers access to a broader range of products and services the buyer can offer their consumers at more attractive costs.

Other ST liabilities
These are short-term debts that don't cause interest expenses. For example, they might be loans from founders or accrued taxes (taxes owed, already incurred, but not yet paid).

Outlays
Net disbursements (cash payments in excess of cash receipts) for administrative expenses and for loans and related costs and expenses (e.g., gross disbursements for loans and expenses minus loan repayments, interest and fee income collected, and reimbursements received for services performed for other agencies).

Outsourcing
Purchasing an item or a service from an outside vendor to replace performance of the task with an organization's internal operations.

Paid-in capital
Real money paid into the company as investments. This is not to be confused with par value of stock, or market value of stock. This is actual money paid into the company as equity investments by owners.

Partnership
Partnerships are harder to describe because they change so much. They are governed by state laws, but a Uniform Partnership Act that has become the law in most states. That act, however, mostly sets the specific partnership agreement as the real legal core of the partnership, so the legal details can vary widely. Usually the income or loss from partnerships pass through to the partners, without any partnership tax. The agreements can define different levels of risk, which is why you'll read about some partnerships that have general partners and limited partners, with different levels of risk for each. The agreement should also define what happens if a partner withdraws, buy and sell arrangements for partners, and liquidation arrangements if that becomes necessary. If you think a partnership might work for your business, make sure you do this right. Find an attorney with experience in partnerships, and check for references of present and past clients. This is a complicated area and a mistake in the agreement will cause a lot of problems.

Patent
A patent secures to an inventory the exclusive right to make, use and sell an invention for 17 years. Inventors should contact the U.S. Department of Commerce Patent Office.

Payback period
The number of years required for an organization to recapture an initial investment. This may apply to an entire business operation or an individual project.

Payment days
The average number of days that pass between receiving an invoice and paying it. It is not a simple estimate; it is calculated with a financial formula:
=(Accounts payable balance*360)/(Total entries to accounts payable*12)

Payroll burden
Payroll burden includes payroll taxes and benefits. It is calculated using a percentage assumption that is applied to payroll. For example, if payroll is $1,000 and the burden rate is 10 percent, the burden is an extra $100. Acceptable payroll burden rates vary by market, by industry, and by company.

Penetration pricing strategy
Setting a relatively low initial price for a new product or service.

Perceived risk
The extent to which a customer or client is uncertain about the consequences of an action, often relating to purchase decisions.

Perceptual map
A two or three-dimensional illustration of customer's perceptions of competing products comparing select attributes based on market research.

Personal selling
The use of face-to-face communication between the seller and buyer.

Personnel burden
Payroll burden. See above description.

GLOSSARY OF BUSINESS TERMS

PEST Analysis
Political, Economic, and Social Trends
PEST is a popular framework for situation analysis, looking at political, economic, and social trends. Analyzing these factors can help generate marketing ideas, product ideas, etc.

Plant and equipment
This is the same as long-term, fixed, or capital assets.

Point of purchase (POP) advertising
A retail in-store presentation that displays product and communicates information to retail consumers at the place of purchase.

Positioning
Orchestrating an organization's offering and image to occupy a unique and valued place in the customer's mind relative to competitive offerings. A product or service can be positioned on the basis of an attribute or benefit, use or application, user, class, price, or quality.

Percentage Lease
Base rent, operating expenses, common area maintenance, plus percentage of tenant's gross income (most common for retailers in shopping malls).

Premiums
A product-oriented promotion that offers some free or reduced-price item contingent on the purchase of advertised or featured merchandise or service.

Price elasticity of demand
The change in demand relative to a change in price for a product or service.

Prime rate
Interest rate which is charged business borrowers having the highest credit ratings, for short term borrowing.

PRO-Net
An Internet-based database of information of small, disadvantaged, 8(a) and women-owned businesses seeking procurement contracts.

Product liability
Type of tort or civil liability that applies to product manufacturers and sellers.

Professional and trade associations
Non-profit, cooperative and voluntary organizations that are designed to help their members in dealing with problems of mutual interest. In many instances professional and trade associations enter into an agreement with SBA to provide volunteer counseling to the small business community.

Pro forma income statement
A projected Income Statement. Pro forma in this context means projected. An income statement is the same as a profit and loss statement, a financial statement that shows sales, cost of sales, gross margin, operating expenses, and profits.

Pro Forma statements
Financial statements that project the results of future business operations. Examples include a pro forma balance sheet, a pro forma income statement, and a pro forma cash flow statement.

Product definition
A stage in a new product development process in which concepts are translated into actual products for additional testing based on interactions with customers.

Product development
Expenses incurred in development of new products (salaries, laboratory equipment, test equipment, prototypes, research and development, etc.).

Product development strategy
A product-market strategy whereby an organization creates new offerings for existing markets innovation, product augmentation, or product line extensions.

Product life cycle (PLC)
The phases of the sales projections or history of a product or service category over time used to assist with marketing mix decisions and strategic options available. The four stages of the product life cycle include introduction, growth, maturity, and decline, and typically follow a predictable pattern based on sales volume over a period of time.

Product line
A group of closely related products with similar attributes or target markets.

Product-line pricing
The setting of prices for all items in a product line involving the lowest-priced product price, the highest price product, and price differentials for all other products in the line.

Profit
Profit is an accounting concept, normally the bottom line of the Income Statement, which is also called Profit or Loss statement. Start with sales, subtract all costs of sales and all expenses, and that produces profit before tax. Subtract tax to get net profit.

Profit before interest and taxes
This is also called EBIT, for Earnings Before Interest and Taxes. It is gross margin minus operating expenses.

Profit or loss
Also called Profit and Loss statement. An income statement is a financial statement that shows sales, cost of sales, gross margin, operating expenses, and profits or losses. Gross margin is sales less cost of sales, and profit (or loss) is gross margin less operating expenses and taxes. The result is profit if it's positive, loss if it's negative.

Proprietorship
The most common legal form of business ownership; about 85 percent of all small businesses are proprietorships. The liability of the owner is unlimited in this form of ownership.

Protest
A statement in writing by any bidder or offeror on a particular procurement alleging that another bidder or offeror on such procurement is not a small business concern.

Public relations
Communications often in the form of news distributed in a non-personal form which may include newspaper, magazine, radio, television, Internet or other form of media for which the sponsoring organization does not pay a fee.

Pull communication strategy
The practice of creating interest among potential buyers, who then demand the offering from intermediaries, ultimately "pulling" the offering through the channel.

Push communication strategy
The practice of "pushing" an offering through a marketing channel in a sequential fashion, with each channel focusing on a distinct target market. The principal emphasis is on personal selling and trade promotions directed toward wholesalers and retailers

Questionable costs
Costs that may be considered as variable or as fixed costs, depending on the specifics of the situation.

Ratio
Denotes relationships of items within and between financial statements, e.g., current ratio, quick ratio, inventory turnover ratio and debt/net worth ratios.

Receivables turnover
Sales on credit for an accounting period divided by the average accounts receivables balance.

Regional marketing
The practice of using different marketing mixes to accommodate unique preferences and competitive conditions in different geographical areas.

Relevant cost
Expenditures that are expected to occur in the future as a result of some marketing action and differ among other potential marketing alternatives.

Repositioning
The process of strategically changing the perceptions surrounding a product or service.

Request for Proposals
Solicitations for offerings for competitive negotiated procurements when it is impossible to draft an invitation for bids containing adequate detailed description of the required property and services. There are 15 circumstances in the Federal Acquisition Regulations (FAR) which permit negotiated procurements.

Retained earnings
Earnings (or losses) that have been reinvested into the company, not paid out as dividends to the owners. When retained earnings are negative, the company has accumulated losses.

Return on assets
Net profits divided by total assets. A measure of profitability.

Return on investment
[1]Net profits divided by net worth or total equity; yet another measure of profitability. [2]The ability of a given investment to earn a return for its use. Also called ROI.

Return on sales
Net profits divided by sales; another measure of profitability.

Rich-Gumpert Evaluation System
A method of analysis that associates a numeric value between 1 and 4 regarding the spectrums of product development and the entrepreneur and management team. For example, the most desirable "4/4" rating represents a fully developed product with an established market that is supported by a fully staffed and experienced management team.

Right of first refusal
Before vacant space is rented to someone else, landlord must offer it to the current tenant with the same terms that will be offered to the public.

Rogers, Everett
Author who studied and published information on the theory of diffusion of innovation.
ROI
Return on investment; net profits divided by net worth or total equity, another measure of profitability.

S Corporation (S Corp)
Corporations are either the standard C corporation or the small business S corporation. The C corporation is the classic legal entity of the vast majority of successful companies in the United States. Most lawyers would agree that the C corporation is the structure that provides the best shielding from personal liability for owners, and provides the best non-tax benefits to owners. This is a separate legal entity, different from its owners, which pays its own taxes. Most lawyers would also probably agree that for a company that has ambitions of raising major investment capital and eventually going public, the C corporation is the standard form of legal entity. The S corporation is used for family companies and smaller ownership groups. The clearest distinction from C is that the S corporation's profits or losses go straight through to the S corporation's owners, without being taxed separately first. In practical terms, this means that the owners of the corporation can take their profits home without first paying the corporation's separate tax on profits, so those profits are taxed once for the S owner, and twice for the C owner. In practical terms the C corporation doesn't send its profits home to its owners as much as the S corporation does, because it usually has different goals and objectives. It often wants to grow and go public, or it already is public. In most states an S corporation is owned by a limited number (25 is a common maximum) of private owners, and corporations can't hold stock in S corporations, just individuals. Corporations can switch from C to S and back again, but not often. The IRS has strict rules for when and how those switches are made. You'll almost always want to have your CPA and in some cases your attorney guide you through the legal requirements for switching.

Sales break-even
The sales volume at which costs are exactly equal to sales. The exact formula is:
=Fixed costs/[1 - (Unit Variable Cost/Unit Price)]

GLOSSARY OF BUSINESS TERMS ●●●●●●

Sales forecast
The level of sales a single organization expects to achieve based on a chosen marketing strategy and assumed competitive environment.

Sales on credit
Sales made on account; shipments against invoices to be paid later.

Scrambled merchandising
The practice by wholesalers and retailers that carry an increasingly wider assortment of merchandise.

Secondary market
Those who purchase an interest in a loan from an original lender, such as banks, institutional investors, insurance companies, credit unions and pension funds.

Seed capital
Seed capital is investment contributed at a very early stage of a new venture, usually in relatively small amounts. It comes even before what they call "first round" venture capital.
How much is that "relatively small amount?" I've heard some high-end high-tech ventures in the heart of Silicon Valley call an investment of $500K seed capital, and I've known of other ventures that called $35K investment seed capital, and the following $300K investment the first round. It depends on the point of view.

Selective distribution
A strategy where a producer sells its products or services in a few exclusively chosen retail outlets in a specific geographical area.

Selling Approaches
Five potential selling resources based on the sales value and the distribution of the product.

Service Corps of Retired Executives (SCORE)
A no-cost consulting and resources service offered by Retired, and working, successful business persons who volunteer to render assistance in counseling, training and guiding small business clients through the Small Business Administration.

Short term
Normally used to distinguish between short-term and long-term, when referring to assets or liabilities. Definitions vary because different companies and accountants handle this in different ways. Accounts payable is always a short-term liability, and cash, accounts receivable and inventory are always short-term assets. Most companies call any debt of less than five-year terms short-term debt. Assets that depreciate over more than five years (e.g., plant and equipment) are usually long-term assets.

Short term assets
Cash, securities, bank accounts, accounts receivable, inventory, business equipment, assets that last less than five years or are depreciated over terms of less than five years. Also called Current Assets.

Short term notes
These are the same as short-term loans. These are debts with terms of five years or less.

Simple Linear Regression
A linear correlation that offers a straight-line projection based on the variables considered.

Situation analysis
The assessment of operations to determine the reasons for the gap between what was or is expected, and what has happened or will happen.

Skimming pricing strategy
Setting a relatively high initial price for a new product or service when there is a strong price-perceived quality relationship that targets early adopters that are price insensitive. The price may be lowered over time.

Slotting allowances
Payments to store chains for acquiring and maintaining shelf space.

Small Business Development Centers (SBDC)
The SBDC is a university-based center for the delivery of joint government, academic, and private sector services for the benefit of small business and the national welfare. It is committed to the development and productivity of business and the economy in specific geographical regions.

Small Business Investment Council (SBIC)
A division of the Small Business Administration that offers "venture capital-like" resources to higher risk businesses seeking capital.

Sole proprietorship
The simplest form is the sole proprietorship. Simply put, your business is a sole proprietorship if you don't create a separate legal entity for it. This is true whether you operate it in your own name, or under a trade name. If it isn't your own name, then you register a company name as a "Fictitious business name," also called a DBA ("Doing Business As"). Depending on your state, you can usually obtain this through the county government, and the cost is no more than a small registration fee plus a required newspaper ad, for a total of less than $100 in most states.

The main disadvantage of the sole proprietorship is the lack of a separate entity, which means you have personal responsibility for it. If the business fails then its creditors can go after your personal assets. Tax treatment is quite simple, your profit and loss goes straight through to your personal taxes. Your business income is normally on Schedule C of your tax return. This can be good or bad for your tax situation, depending on where you stand with other income.

Starting date
The starting date for the entire business plan.

Strategic control
The practice of assessing the direction of the organization as evidenced by its implicit or explicit goals, objectives, strategies, and capacity to perform in the context of changing environmental and competitive actions.

Strategic marketing management
The planned process of defining the organization's business, mission, and goals; identifying and framing organizational opportunities; formulating product-market strategies, budgeting marketing, financial, and production resources; developing reformulation

Sublet
Tenant rents all or part of space to another business; tenant is still responsible for paying all costs to landlord.

Success factors
Primary success factors include considerations regarding: 1) The choice of business based on the status of the market 2) Education and experience 3) People and collaboration 4) Creativity and innovation versus business skills and networks 5) Incubation potential 6) Leveraging available resources 7) Management practices

Success requirements
The basic tasks that must be performed by an organization in a market or industry to compete successfully. These are sometimes "key success factors."

Sunk cost
Past expenditures for a given activity that are typically irrelevant in whole or in part to future decisions. The "sunk cost fallacy" is an attempt to recoup spent dollars by spending still more dollars in the future.

Switching Costs
The costs incurred in changing from one provider of a product or service to another. Switching costs may be tangible or intangible costs incurred due to the change of this source.

SWOT analysis
A formal framework of identifying and framing organizational growth opportunities. SWOT is an acronym for an organization's internal Strengths and Weaknesses and external Opportunities and Threats.

Systematic Innovation
Innovation resulting from an intentional and organized process to evaluate opportunities to introduce change, based on a definition provided by Peter Drucker. The sources of innovation may be internal or external to the enterprise.

Tactics
A collection of tools, activities and business decisions required to implement a strategy.

Target market
The target market is a defined segment of the market that is the strategic focus of a business or a marketing plan. Normally the members of this segment possess common characteristics and a relative high propensity to purchase a particular product or service. Because of this, the member of this segment represent the greatest potential for sales volume and frequency. The target market is often defined in terms of geographic, demographic, and psychographic characteristics.

Target marketing
The process of marketing to a specific market segment or multiple segments. Differentiated target marketing occurs when an organization simultaneously pursues several different market segments, usually with a different strategy for each. Concentrated target marketing occurs when a single market segment is pursued.

Tax rate percent
An assumed percentage applied against pre-tax income to determine taxes.

Taxes incurred
Taxes owed but not yet paid.

Telemarketing
A form of direct marketing that uses the telephone to reach potential customers.

Trade margin
The difference between unit sales price and unit cost and each level of a marketing channel usually expressed in percentage terms.

Trading down
The process of reducing the number of features or quality of an offering to realize a lower purchase price.

Trading up
The practice of improving an offering by adding new features and higher quality materials or adding products or services to increase the purchase price.

Triple net lease
Tenant pays base rent, taxes, insurance, repairs and maintenance.

Turnover (Business)
Turnover is the number of times that an average inventory of goods is sold during a fiscal year or some designated period. Care must be taken to ensure that the average inventory and net sales are both reduced to the same denominator; that is, divide inventory at cost into sales at cost or divide inventory at selling price into sales at selling price. Do not mix cost price with selling price. The turnover when accurately computed, is one measure of the efficiency of a business.

Types of entrepreneurs
Entrepreneurs may be categorized into 11 areas including: 1) Solo self-employed individuals 2) Team builders 3) Independent innovators 4) Pattern multipliers 5) Economy of scale exploiters 6) Capital aggregators 7) Acquires 8) Buy-sell artists 9) Conglomerates 10) Speculators 11) Apparent value manipulators

Undelivered orders
The amount of orders for goods and services outstanding for which, the liability has not yet accrued. For practical purposes represents obligations incurred for which goods have not been delivered or services not performed.

Unfair labor practice
Action by either the employer or union which violates the provisions of EO 11491 as amended.

UI

User Interface. It is the graphic design and appearance of a website, its function as seen and used by the person on the user end, at the website in a browser. The UI of a website is ultimately how it lets users know what it has to offer them. If it lacks an easy navigation scheme users get lost, and never find the information on a site. The full potential of any website is unleashed through the UI.

Uniform commercial code

Codification of uniform laws concerning commercial transactions. In SBA parlance generally refers to a uniform method of recording and enforcing a security interest or charge upon existing or to be acquired personal property.

Unit variable cost

The specific labor and materials associated with a single unit of goods sold. Does not include general overhead.

Units break-even

The unit sales volume at which the fixed and variable costs are exactly equal to sales. The formula is: UBE=Fixed costs/(Unit Price - Unit Variable Cost)

Unpaid expenses

Business Plan Pro uses this term to refer to other short-term liabilities in the Start-up table. Normally these would be expenses incurred with credit cards during the start-up phase, such as expenses for office furniture, fixtures, and equipment. Amounts typed into this cell in the Start-up table become the opening balance for Other Short-term Liabilities in the balance sheet. To pay these amounts when due, enter negative dollar amounts into the corresponding row on the Cash Flow table, the one for "other short-term liabilities."

User Benefits

Understanding and appreciating the base reason an individual purchases a product or service that may not directly correlate with the feature or function of the good or service. These benefits may be intangible.

User Interface (UI)

User Interface. It is the graphic design and appearance of a website, its function as seen and used by the person on the user end, at the website in a browser. The UI of a website is ultimately how it lets users know what it has to offer them. If it lacks an easy navigation scheme users get lost, and never find the information on a site. The full potential of any website is unleashed through the UI.

Usury

Interest which exceeds the legal rate charged to a borrower for the use of money.

Valuation

Used as a noun, Valuation is what a business is worth, as in "this company's valuation is $10 million." This would mean that a company is valued at $10 million, or worth $10 million. The term is used most often for discussions of sale or purchase of a company; its valuation is the price of a share times the number of shares outstanding, and the price of a share is the total valuation divided by the number of shares outstanding.

Some of the different valuation methods consider:

1. Rate of return
2. Timing and form of return
3. Amount of control desired
4. Acceptable level of risk
5. Perception of risk

Standard new venture valuation methods may include:

1. Asset-based valuation: the business is worth the sum of its assets. Not a popular valuation method for new businesses, because their future should be worth a lot more than their assets.
2. Book value: the book value of a company is the calculation of assets less liabilities.
3. Adjusted book value: this variation adjusts the assets - liabilities calculation for real value of assets, distinguished from the accounting value.
4. Liquidation value: what a business would yield in real money if its assets were liquidated.
5. Replacement value: what it would cost to replace the business if the replacement started from scratch.
6. Earnings Based Valuations: this is by far the most popular method for new businesses; they are valued based on future earnings. Valuation is also important for tax reporting. Some tax-related events such as sale, purchase or gifting of shares of a company will be taxed depending on valuation. The term is used less in discussions of major publicly traded companies, but it is essentially the same as market cap or market capitalization.

   Used as a verb, valuation is the process of determining what the business' valuation. In this context, a valuation is like an audit, and a valuation expert is a CPA or analyst who does valuations. Some CPAs are certified as valuation experts, which means the IRS is more likely to accept their valuation as part of a transaction related to taxes.

Value

The ratio of perceived benefits compared to price for a product or service.

Variable Cost

Costs that fluctuate in direct proportion to the volume of units produced. The best and most obvious example are physical costs of goods sold, direct costs, such as materials, products purchased for resale, production costs and overhead, etc. The concept of variable cost is an important component of risk in a company, because generally variable costs are less risky than fixed costs, because variable costs are not incurred unless there are sales and production. See also break-even analysis, fixed costs, contribution

Variance

A calculation of the difference between plan and actual results, used by analysts to manage and track the impact of planning and budgeting.

GLOSSARY OF BUSINESS TERMS

Venture Capital

Venture capital nowadays is used two ways: first, people often take venture capital as any investment capital obtained through private investment or public investment funds directed to high-risk and high-potential enterprises. This funding is provided to new or existing firms that exhibit above-average growth rates, a significant potential for market expansion and the need for additional financing for business maintenance or expansion. Second, within the more informed and sophisticated business circles, venture capital is defined more narrowly as investment money coming from the mainstream venture capital firms, a few hundred major firms, different from investment money from other private investors, angels, etc.

Venture Capitalists (VC)

Venture capitalists are thought of in two ways: first, some people think of any wealthy individual who invests in young companies as a venture capitalist. Second, within the more informed investors, analysts, and entrepreneurs, a venture capitalist is a manager of a mainstream venture capital fund. See Venture Capital

Wholesaler

A channel member that purchases from the producer and supplies to the retailer and primarily performs the function of physical distribution and stocking inventory for rapid delivery.

Word processing

Is the efficient and effective production of written communications at the lowest possible cost through the combined use of systems management procedures, automated technology, and accomplished personnel. The equipment used in word processing applications includes but is not limited to the following: Dictation and transcription equipment, automatic repetitive typewriters, visual display text editing typewriters, keyboard terminals, etc.

Workers' compensation

A state-mandated form of insurance covering workers injured in job- related accidents. In some states the state is the insurer; in other states insurance must be acquired from commercial insurance firms. Insurance rates are based on a number of factors including salaries, firm history and risk of occupation.

Working capital

The accessible resources needed to support the day-to-day operations of an organization. It is commonly in the form of cash and short-term assets including accounts receivable, prepaid expenses, and short-term accounts payable for goods and services, and current unpaid income taxes.

Source: sba.gov, bplans.com

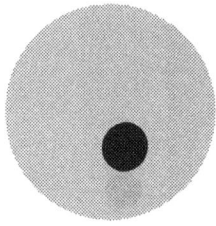

DISCOVERING THE VISION

&

DEVELOPING THE CHARACTER OF A VISIONARY

"For we are His workmanship, created in Christ Jesus for good works, which God prepared beforehand that we should walk in them."
Ephesians 2:10

The Visionary's Source

VISIONEERING by Andy Stanley (Book)

$12.99
(plus tax & shipping & handling)

A magnificent display of how to live a vision-driven life by fulfilling God's purposes through intentional living. It is necessary to have a clear, God-ordained vision for each of the roles in your life. Whether you're a parent with a vision for your children or a CEO pursuing a corporate vision, Visioneering will give you the foundation you need to birth the vision.

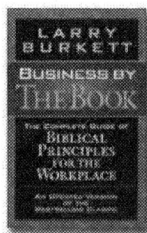

BUSINESS by THE BOOK by Larry Burkett (Book)

$13.99
(plus tax & shipping & handling)

Invest in this bestselling, business-altering book. Business by the Book is a step-by-step presentation of how to operate your business according to the Ultimate Businessman. Discover what God's word says about forming partnerships and corporations, hiring and firing decisions, borrowing and lending decisions, and business tithing requirements.

I LAY HOLD (4-Tape Series)

$20.00
(plus tax & shipping & handling)

Not a 3-peat but a 4-peat compilation from four futuring leaders in our midst; Pastor Waymond Burton, Water of Life Christian Church, Greenville, SC, Apostle Ron Carpenter, Redemption World Outreach Center, Greenville, SC, Bishop Waymond Burton, Zina Christian Center, Raleigh, NC, and Pastor Curtis Johnson, Valley Brook Outreach Baptist Church, Greenville, SC. Each message reveals that God is calling us to "press" as Apostle Paul pressed noted in Philippians 3:12 when he said "Not that I have already attained, or am already perfected; but I press on, that I may lay hold of that for which Christ Jesus has also laid hold of me." Be strengthened and encouraged to press towards your destiny in Christ Jesus!

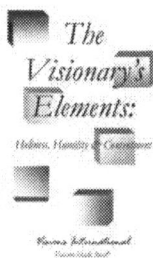

THE VISIONARY'S ELEMENTS: HOLINESS, HUMILITY & CONTENTMENT (3-Tape Series)

$15.00
(plus tax & shipping & handling)

Element is defined as a natural habitat or environment; the basic and most important things to be learned when studying a subject. In the character and quality of a visionary is woven a godly reverence to be holy, humble, and content. These essential elements keep the visionary in proper relationship with God, themselves and others. Pastor Camille Burton of Water of Life Christian Church will lead you through an exploration of the facets of each element. Learn how God has equipped each of us to walk holy, humble, and content before Him and others.

More Titles Available!
From authors such as . . .

- John Maxwell – "Developing the Leader Within You" and "21 Indispensable Qualities of a Leader"
- Mike Murdock – "The Secrets of the Richest Man Who Ever Lived" and "31 Secrets of an Unforgettable Women"
- Kenneth Blanchard – "Who Moved My Cheese" and "The One Minute Manager"

And that's not it . . . Request a full listing today!

The Visionary's Source ●●●●●●

THE VISIONARY'S GUIDE to SMALL BUSINESS DEVELOPMENT
(Step-by-Step-Guide)(National) **$59.95**
(plus tax & shipping & handling)

Vision International's compilation of 4 years of research and development on small business establishment. In one guide, find solutions to the daunting task of small business development. Complete with explanations on writing vision and mission statements, financial statements, bookkeeping, goal mapping, an exhaustive business start-up checklist, legal formation options, and tax incentives, business forms, local, state and federal regulations directory, a glossary of business terms and more!

State Specific Guide Available for:
South Carolina and Georgia **$79.95**

Includes all of the above plus forms and directories downloaded (plus tax & shipping & handling)
directly from your state and local governement.

THE VISIONARY'S NOTES (Notebook) **$8.50**
(plus tax & shipping & handling)

Compile all your scattered notes by using these forms provided for quarterly planning, future planning, goal mapping, company, product, customer, and competitor analyses, task lists, phone directory, web directory and more!

✂ -

Six Ways to Pay:

❑ Cash, Check or Money Order
Payable to *Visions International*
Your name must be preprinted on the Check.
Returned Checks are subject to a service charges of $30.00

❑ VISA ❑ [MasterCard] ❑ [card]

Card # _____ Expiration Date _____

Signature as appears on credit card _____

Printed Name as appears on credit card _____

Address 1 _____

Address 2 _____

Phone _____

Email _____

What Would You Like?

Item Name	Qty	Price	Total
		Subtotal	
		5% Tax	
		Shipping	
		Total Due	

Four Ways to Order:

Phone 864.294.1974
E-Fax 512.727.9504
Email king@visionsmadereal.com
Mail Post Office Box 14201
Greenville, SC 29610

Sorry, all sales are final. No refunds or exchanges.

I would like to know more about
Visions International
and the benefits of having a
Business Coach

Name   _____

Address   _____

                 _____

                 _____

Phone 1   _____

Phone 2   _____

Email   _____

Web Address   _____

If Applicable:

Company Name   _____

Type of Business   _____

I'm not in business but I'm interested in starting a business in _____

❑   Yes, please add me to your mailing list to receive the quarterly newsletter, workshop and conference announcements and other information.

Comments welcomed:

_____

_____

Send to:
Bernell L. King
Post Office Box 14201
Greenville, SC 29610
Office 864.294.1974
E-Fax 512.727.9504
Email: king@visionsmadereal.com

Visions Made Real^{SM}

www.ingramcontent.com/pod-product-compliance
Lightning Source LLC
Chambersburg PA
CBHW081504200326
41518CB00015B/2368